The Heart of a Shepherd

"I am the good shepherd; the good shepherd lays down His life for the sheep"
(John 10:11).

Joe White

David was known as *"the man after **God's** own heart."*
"The Heart of A Shepherd"
is a *daily* walk through the
Psalms *of* David to *guide*
a believer to
pursue that **heart**
and become equipped
to give that **heart** away through *discipleship* to others.

The 23rd Psalm

The Lord, the Psalmist's Shepherd.

A Psalm of David.

The Lord is my shepherd,

I shall not want.

He makes me lie down in green pastures;

He leads me beside quiet waters.

He restores my soul;

He guides me in the paths of righteousness

For His name's sake.

Even though I walk through the valley of the shadow of death,

I fear no evil, for You are with me;

Your rod and Your staff, they comfort me.

You prepare a table before me in the presence of my enemies;

You have anointed my head with oil;

My cup overflows.

Surely goodness and lovingkindness will follow me all the days of my life,

And I will dwell in the house of the Lord forever.

Shepherd	רועה	Βοσκός (Voskós)
English	*Hebrew*	*Greek*

shepherd

Noun

shep·herd | \ˈshe-pərd \

Definition of *shepherd*
1: a person who tends sheep
2: a member of the clergy who provides spiritual care and guidance for a congregation

Flock	להקה	σμήνος (smínos)
English	*Hebrew*	*Greek*

flock

Noun

\ˈfläk \
Definition of *flock*
1: a group of animals (such as birds or sheep) assembled or herded together
2: a group of students or children in someone's charge

Lamb	טלה	αρνάκι (arnáki)
English	*Hebrew*	*Greek*

lamb

Noun

\ˈlam \

Definition of *lamb*

1: a young sheep

2: used figuratively as a symbol of meekness, gentleness, or innocence

↳ quality of heart! willing to submit and desire of someone else

Table of Contents

David's 23rd Song

- By Joe White

VERSE 1

You are my Shepherd, I take Your lead,

Beyond Your love, I have no need.

In pastures green, you lay me down,

By peaceful waters Your voice is found.

CHORUS

You are my Shepherd, I want no more,

Your love secure, my soul restore.

You are my Shepherd, I find my rest,

Eternal Lord, Your name I bless.

VERSE 2

Through faith and trust, my soul restored,

I know my Shepherd, He is my Lord.

Along the pathway of righteousness,

Jehovah God, Your name I bless.

BRIDGE

Restore my soul, O Shepherd King,

You fill my cup, Your name I sing.

To you, O Lord, my life I bring,

My soul restored, this song I sing.

VERSE 3

With You my Shepherd, Your rod and staff,

Your hand of comfort, I find my path.

Before my eyes, You prepare my table,

Tho' enemies surround, my God is able.

CHORUS

You are my Shepherd, I want no more,

Your love secure, my soul restore.

You are my Shepherd, I find my rest,

Eternal Lord, Your name I bless.

VERSE 4

Anointing oil, above my head,

My cup overflowing, in abundance fed.

By grace and goodness, You'll leave me never,

Your heavenly home, I'll dwell forever.

BRIDGE

Restore my soul, O Shepherd King,

You fill my cup, Your name I sing.

To You, O Lord, my life I bring,

My soul restored, this song I sing.

David, the Man after God's own Heart

- By Joe White

When Samuel was commissioned by God to travel,
To the house of Jesse, his calling to unravel.

To find a King for Israel his quest,
A man of integrity, God's name to attest.

For Saul's disobedience a replacement was needed,
God's Spirit withdrawn, his anointing defeated.

Go make your sacrifice, The Lord commanded,
In Bethlehem town, the blood demanded.

There consecrate Jesse and all of his sons,
For they have found favor, My chosen ones.

First Eliab, the eldest as Samuel directed,
Though handsome his appearance, yet the Lord rejected.

It's not by might nor power, My selection,
But only by My Spirit do I grant My affection.

Then Abinadab and his brothers each made their appeal,
Yet God refusing, His choice to reveal.

There must be another, Samuel patiently awaited,
Just a lad tending sheep, his heart understated.

As David was presented the prophet was affirmed,
The anointing was given, the youngest confirmed.

As the Spirit of God from Saul departed,
And the favor of God unto David imparted. →came on

13

Then off to the battlefield, an invitation to fight,
From Goliath and the Philistines Saul's fury to incite.

With ridicule and blasphemy, the giant he taunted,
His size, his power, his dominance he flaunted.

For Saul and his army not one took the dare,
Not one would step forward, the giant to forbear.

But David, appalled that none would defend,
The holiness of Jehovah, His name to offend.

David's faith and his slingshot were all that he needed,
With courage and a stone, the giant he defeated.

A new king, people shouted, it was easy to tell,
Saul's heart became jealous the day the giant fell.

The people loved David, his favor multiplied,
Now a guest in Saul's palace and a place by his side.

With Jonathan, Saul's son, a covenant was made,
Their love for each other, true friendship displayed.

Their armor exchanged, now with mutual protection,
Two hearts knit as one, embracing godly affection.

Saul plotted David's murder, with a spear he would fall,
In the palace he'd seize him and pin him to the wall.

But Jonathan told David of the sinister intention,
Given plans for escape with divine intervention.

Saul continued his pursuit, though continually disappointed,
Disenchanted exploitation with the one God anointed.

Yes, twice David secured his own retribution,
Yet denying his flesh and his nemesis' retribution.

> 72. → punishment on someone for wrong or criminal act. as vengeance

To Saul grace was given, David's loyalty unshakable,
A kingdom riveted by his faithfulness unbreakable.

God's covenant with David, his descendants and his throne,
His kingdom forever, his name would be known.

As general of God's Army, no enemy could stand,
Til all foes were conquered under David's command.

Yet David couldn't defeat the father of lies,
For Bathsheba, his sin with the lust of his eyes.

First seduction, then murder, David's certain condemnation,
His spirit overtaken by his fleshly sensation.

Great turmoil in his family, the shadow of his sin,
The death of his child from his corruption within.

Yet God in His mercy, His servant restored,
David fasted, repented, and returned to his Lord.

For the rest of his life David's anthems he'd raise,
Writing songs for the ages enveloped with praise.

The psalms of David, his wisdom to impart.
For David was a man after God's own heart.

From his loins would come One, The Messiah his story,
Through Christ, Son of David, God's eternal glory.

My Sheep Hear My Voice

"My sheep hear My voice, and I know them, and they follow Me" (John 10:27).

"How blessed is the man who does not walk in the counsel of the wicked, nor stand in the path of sinners, nor sit in the seat of scoffers! But his delight is in the law of the Lord, and in His law he meditates day and night" (Psalm 1:1-2).

Psalm 1

The Oxford Dictionary defines the word *communication* as "the successful conveying or sharing of ideas and feelings." If a thought or an idea from an outside source doesn't sound like the Bible, it probably is not God's voice.

Imagine the awe-inspiring thought that God is 100 percent love, 100 percent wise, and 100 percent concerned for your ultimate good. His scriptural words are given to guide you, to inspire you, and to empower you to do His will. Little wonder, then, that Psalm 138 states, *"All the kings of the earth will give thanks to You, O Lord, when they have heard the words of Your mouth."* To meditate on His Word is to use the paintbrush of wisdom to paint your heart the color of His. To hear His voice is to understand His will and purpose for your life. → taking the time to understand! under

There are approximately 7,100 living languages in the world. Meditating on Scripture is learning the language of God.

1) Where in today's world do you find the counsel of the wicked, the ⤷ really like that! path of sinners, and the seat of scoffers? ⤷ to follow certain ways ⤷ destroy others deny good things
   I find that with social media destroying our minds and taking in social pressures and life of college students

   As you listen to today's music, watch most TV and movies, and participate in the worst parts of social media, how is that instructing your mind in the language of "the world, the flesh, and the devil"?
   the negative talk especially saying "OMG" (oh my god), god damn, saying the lords name in vain, cursing is also a huge one today.

   Bilingual people have a "primary language," usually from the place where they live and spend the majority of their time. All believers are bilingual; they speak the language of the flesh and the language of God. What is your primary language? How do you know?
   I would say my primary language is of GOD because I've been really trying to base my actions on him. I can really improve on that though.

2) **Psalm 1:2a -** *"But his delight is in the law of the Lord."* How do you define the word *delight*?
   something good! saturate yourself with, be all into something enjoyable and positive like GOD!

   What is the difference between *duty* and *delight*? → spend more time in.
   duty is something we need to do delight is something we get to do delight tends to be more enjoyable sometimes. enjoy something vs. doing something

17

3) **John 14:23** - *"Jesus answered and said to him, 'If anyone loves Me, he will keep My word; and My Father will love him, and We will come to him and make Our abode with him.'"*

What is the difference between simply "hearing" the Shepherd's call and "keeping" His Word?

hearing you follow him and almost do something, but keeping it is using his word to navigate your life not just to do one specific thing once.

4) **Psalm 1:2b** - *"And in His law he meditates day and night."*

What are some ways you can practically meditate on His Word "day and night"?

I can write bible verses around dorm room and on supplies to constantly remind me! spend time in the word directly!

or listening to learning talks about that

5) **Psalm 1:3** - *"He will be like a tree firmly planted by streams of water, which yields its fruit in its season and its leaf does not wither; and in whatever he does, he prospers."*

What is God's promise to the person who meditates on His Word day and night?

That they will prosper in with and be strong in everything they do!

THE SHEPHERD'S CALL

6) **John 13:15** - *"For I gave you an example that you also should do as I did to you."*

From today's passage, how does **THE** Shepherd inspire **you** to shepherd **your** flock?

continue to read and meditate on his work and really take the time to delight in things, also be more concious of the words I'm saying

MINUTE OF MEDITATION

"But his delight is in the law of the Lord, and in His law he meditates day and night" (Psalm 1:2).

PRAYER

Adoration, **C**onfession, **T**hanksgiving, **S**upplication

asking

↳Admiring

18

Worshipping the Shepherd

"Now therefore, O kings, show discernment; take warning, O judges of the earth. Worship the Lord with reverence and rejoice with trembling"
(Psalm 2:10-11).

Psalm 2

Charles Wesley took this exhortation seriously. Indeed, he worshipped the Shepherd with almost every breath that entered his lungs. Wesley wrote 8,989 hymns by writing an average of 10 lines of verse every day for 50 years. His songs of praise included such favorites as "Christ the Lord Is Risen Today," "Hark! the Herald Angels Sing," and "O for a Thousand Tongues to Sing." Adoration, admiration, and appreciation are the bedrocks on which worship stands. Praise, thanksgiving, and biblically focused singing are the pillars of worshipful expression.

A truly reverent God-worshipper will think worshipfully, talk worshipfully, and live worshipfully, expressing his or her heart of praise in work, study, recreation, entertainment, and in times of solitude. Your mind, your heart, and your emotions are God's gifts to you. Directing them back to their Creator is *your* gift to God. → giving thanks, coming back to him. → doing alone

1) **Isaiah 25:1** - *"O Lord, You are my God; I will exalt You, I will give thanks to Your name; for You have worked wonders, plans formed long ago, with perfect faithfulness."* →?

   How does God's faithfulness inspire the depth of your soul to lift your heart in worship?

   God's faithfulness in knowing that he's got everything under control & for our best interest wants to have me worship as he takes on my stress.

2) **Psalm 63:1** - *"O God, You are my God; I shall seek You earnestly; my soul thirsts for You, my flesh yearns for You, in a dry and weary land where there is no water."* & worries of life ?

   And I want to build on relationship!

   How does this beloved passage inspire your worship as you remember how God met you in your greatest times of desperation?

   He is always there for us no matter what, we should always go to God first! Worship the lord as he has always been there for me.

3) **Habakkuk 3:17-18** - *"Though the fig tree should not blossom and there be no fruit on the vines, though the yield of the olive should fail and the fields produce no food, though the flock should be cut off from the fold and there be no cattle in the stalls, yet I will exult in the Lord, I will rejoice in the God of my salvation."* → ?

   How does this passage influence your devotion to God in worship, even in times when God is literally *all* you have to cling to?

   God will always be there and he is worth spending the time to get to know him. You want to have a great relationship, the more time you spend the closer you feel!

19

4) **2 Corinthians 1:3-4** - *"Blessed be the God and Father of our Lord Jesus Christ, the Father of mercies and God of all comfort, who comforts us in all our affliction so that we will be able to comfort those who are in any affliction with the comfort with which we ourselves are comforted by God."*

What does this passage teach you about the Shepherd you worship and His forward-thinking plan for your life?

That how God loves and teaches us we should take that and use it to love and teach others in our future.

5) **James 3:10** - *"... from the same mouth come both blessing and cursing. My brethren, these things ought not to be this way."*

This passage is meant to search out, identify, and exhort you to erase hypocrisy and double-mindedness in your worship. How well are you cooperating in that process?

I think I am kinda struggling oh! need to stop saying with this at the moment! really struggling to understand deeply & not be ashamed to

6) **Matthew 4:10** - *"Then Jesus said to him, 'Go, Satan! For it is written, "You shall worship the Lord your God, and serve Him only."'"* *go by my- self!*

What is Jesus' firm command in this passage saying to you?

There is only one God and he is our almighty and amazing lord! he is so so good! Trust in him! → with everything

THE SHEPHERD'S CALL

7) **John 13:15** - *"For I gave you an example that you also should do as I did to you."*

From today's scripture, how does **THE** Shepherd inspire **you** to shepherd **your** flock?

Be someone who practices what they say and do all thing for the glory of God and with God in a way thats a light to others and someone who is trying to be more like Jesus!

MINUTE OF MEDITATION

"Worship the Lord with reverence and rejoice with trembling" (Psalm 2:11).

PRAYER

Adoration, **C**onfession, **T**hanksgiving, **S**upplication

The Shepherd, Our Defender

"Truly, truly, I say to you, he who does not enter by the door into the fold of the sheep, but climbs up some other way, he is a thief and a robber" (John 10:1).

Psalm 3

The successful football coach knows the best offense is a good defense. The mission of the defense is to protect your goal line from your opponent's aggression. The best way to prepare for a football game is to study the tactics of your opponent by watching film from his previous performances.

As it is in football, so it is in life. The adversary of our soul is in relentless pursuit of our demise in life and eternity. His attacks are repeated endlessly through the lust of our eyes and the bitterness, fear, and anxiety of our hearts. Our *only* sure defense is the great defender of our souls: Jesus, our Shepherd and Warrior for our eternal salvation.

1) **Psalm 3:1** - *"O Lord, how my adversaries have increased! Many are rising up against me."* Also satan I feel has been → increasing anxiety w/ portfolio examination &

   How has Satan come after you recently, and how has God delivered comparing my work you? ← to others
   Recently with feeling like no belonging and wanting something from a church but through a serman that it's what is taught

2) **Psalm 3:3** - *"But You, O Lord, are a shield about me."* there the most important given

   Describe your dependence on your Shepherd for your personal move protection and revival during times of pain and persecution. confidence in myself
   I really depend on him in prayer and recently asking to just help me get through the day & taking one step @ a time

3) **Psalm 3:5-6** - *"I lay down and slept; I awoke, for the Lord sustains me.* not *I will not be afraid of ten thousands of people."* just tackle everything @ once!

   What is one way the enemy tries to defeat you? How well do you cooperate with the power of your Shepherd to withstand the enemy's attack?
   Telling me I'm not good enough, I try to cooperate w/ the shepherd power to sustain attack but not always need to focus on written

4) **Psalm 3:7** - *"Arise, O Lord; save me, O my God! For You have smitten* written *all my enemies on the cheek; You have shattered the teeth of the* truth! *wicked."*

   Since you originally trusted Jesus, have you developed this same kind of confidence in His care for you? How has He protected you?
   yes, I know he cares for me so much and wants to have a plan layed out for my life. He has protected me from hurtful people & help reduce my anxiety specifically stomach anxiety!

21

5) **Psalm 3:8 -** *"Salvation belongs to the Lord; Your blessing be upon Your people!"*

Put your appreciation for your Shepherd's hand of protection into words.

I need GOD he keeps me on track and protected from things that come my way! he's there through everything

6) **1 Peter 2:24-25 -** *"And He Himself bore our sins in His body on the cross, so that we might die to sin and live to righteousness; for by His wounds you were healed. For you were continually straying like sheep, but now you have returned to the Shepherd and Guardian of your souls."*

Describe how the Great Shepherd has brought you back safely to the flock when you've been lured away by the enemy.

I have been lured away many times but one with watching porn! he really had the Holy spirit inside me making me feel guilty & I prayed and he has brought me back to purity w/! mat!.

THE SHEPHERD'S CALL

7) **John 13:15 -** *"For I gave you an example that you also should do as I did to you."*

From today's scripture, how does **THE** Shepherd inspire **you** to shepherd **your** flock?

to show how I let god dictate and take control & how I love and trust in him as my defender!

MINUTE OF MEDITATION
"But You, O Lord, are a shield about me, my glory, and the One who lifts my head" (Psalm 3:3).

PRAYER
Adoration, Confession, Thanksgiving, Supplication

Crying Out to the Shepherd

"Truly, truly, I say to you, he who does not enter by the door into the fold of the sheep, but climbs up some other way, he is a thief and a robber"
(John 10:1).

Psalm 4

One cold and rainy night, a dear friend found a two- or three-day-old fawn, lost and probably dying, in a drainage ditch. My friend knew of my heart for wounded and orphaned animals and came to me with the wet, shivering, helpless, spotted doe. I warmed a bottle of goat milk and tried to place it in the terrified baby deer's mouth. The fawn let out a deafening cry of horror as, drop by drop, I forced the healing formula into her system.

Three days later, the little, spotted girl was following me like a puppy dog and downing bottles of life-giving milk like a hungry child. Four months later, I set her free to join the wild herd that lives in the woods near my house.

1) **Psalm 4:1** - *"Answer me when I call, O God of my righteousness! You have relieved me in my distress; be gracious to me and hear my prayer."*

   Like the cry of a young whitetail in distress, the cry of a lamb is deafening. It's an outcry that only a loving parent with the milk of life can satisfy. Jesus is *our* loving Shepherd. When was your outcry to Him the most deafening?

   probably when it came to my testing anxiety & with people.

   How did He meet your need in that distress?

   He helped me to regain confidence and calmness into me, helped me to find fitting roommates!

2) **Psalm 4:2** - *"O sons of men, how long will my honor become a reproach? How long will you love what is worthless and aim at deception?"*

   What is David proclaiming about our patterns of sin, and how do those patterns affect our relationship with God?

   we continue to commit the same sin over and over again and we aren't honoring the lord & I believe it worsens our relationship w/ him!

3) **Psalm 4:3** - *"But know that the Lord has set apart the godly man for Himself; the Lord hears when I call to Him."*

   What does it mean to be "set apart" from the herd by the Shepherd and to follow Him into places of worth, worship, woundedness, and witness that other sheep are not asked to travel?

   that we follow the lord & are believers so we are able to experience this whole other aspect of life & freedom that sadly other people don't!

4) **John 14:13-14** - *"Whatever you ask in My name, that will I do, so that the Father may be glorified in the Son. If you ask Me anything in My name, I will do it."*

What would Jesus have you ask for today as you cry out to Him?

A Heart more on fire and determination for the lord & confidence and stress free as I'm putting portfolio above way to many things in my life.

THE SHEPHERD'S CALL

5) **John 13:15** - *"For I gave you an example that you also should do as I did to you."*

From today's scripture, how does **THE** Shepherd inspire **you** to shepherd **your** flock?

Trusting in the lord and living a glorifying to GOD life! Being a light in my daily actions to others.

MINUTE OF MEDITATION
"But know that the Lord has set apart the godly man for Himself; the Lord hears when I call to Him" (Psalm 4:3).

PRAYER
Adoration, **C**onfession, **T**hanksgiving, **S**upplication

The Enemy of the Flock

"Truly, truly, I say to you, he who does not enter by the door into the fold of the sheep, but climbs up some other way, he is a thief and a robber"
(John 10:1).

Psalm 5

There are a million reasons I hate porn. The entire industry is wretched. While using helpless and deluded young women, often sex-trafficked against their will, the proprietors all line their pockets with thousand-dollar bills. In the process, they create sex addicts out of children who carelessly log in on a smartphone or computer. To say porn is the worst drug ever invented is a drastic understatement.

The truth that porn comes straight out of the nostrils of Satan is equally clear. Porn is instantly addictive. Porn creates pictures that never leave the mind of the user. Porn degrades women. Porn disenfranchises wedding vows. Porn leads to worse forms of degradation. Porn turns honeymoons into horror shows. Porn destroys marriages. Porn creates slavery. Only the Shepherd can set the captive free. Only *the* Shepherd can empower the sheep to walk in the pasture of purity and safety.

1) **Psalm 5:1-2 -** *"Give ear to my words, O Lord, consider my groaning. Heed the sound of my cry for help, my King and my God, for to You I pray."*

   How does prayer unlock the door to the pasture of freedom, safety, and security for the sheep? ⤷ never really thought of it like that!
   Because your going to God for help and he is the one who can give pasture of freedom, ana security, safety!

2) **Psalm 5:3 -** *"In the morning, O Lord, You will hear my voice; in the morning I will order my prayer to You and eagerly watch."*

   Why is it essential to begin the day with prayer and Scripture meditation?
   Because it sets your day on the right path and success! GOD should always come first!

3) **Psalm 5:4-6 -** *"For You are not a God who takes pleasure in wickedness; no evil dwells with You. The boastful shall not stand before Your eyes; You hate all who do iniquity. You destroy those who speak falsehood; the Lord abhors the man of bloodshed and deceit."*

   Psalm 101:3 - *"I will set no worthless thing before my eyes; I hate the work of those who fall away; it shall not fasten its grip on me."*
   While the Shepherd gives grace to all who trust in Him, what must our attitude toward sin be if we want to walk in close fellowship with Him?
   we must really not like and resist and turn away from sin not letting it be seen, noticed, or tempting to you. get far away, @ all costs!

Why is a mind continually bathed in the Word the only path of safety and protection for the sheep who follow the Shepherd?

Because its coming from what god is wanting & telling us to do and the spirit ~~is inside them~~ & they know what god would say

4) **Psalm 5:7-8** - *"But as for me, by Your abundant lovingkindness I will enter Your house, at Your holy temple I will bow in reverence for You. O Lord, lead me in Your righteousness because of my foes; make Your way straight before me."* _I can be w/ him_

2 Corinthians 10:5 - *"We are destroying speculations and every lofty thing raised up against the knowledge of God, and we are taking every thought captive to the obedience of Christ."*

How does a believer keep his or her path straight and unblemished?

they are taking everything to the lord and are constantly being filled w/ the word & obeying the lord!

5) **Psalm 5:11-12** - *"But let all who take refuge in You be glad, let them ever sing for joy; and may You shelter them, that those who love Your name may exult in You. For it is You who blesses the righteous man, O Lord, You surround him with favor as with a shield."*

Describe your personal dependence on the Shepherd and the gladness of your heart for His hand of guidance and protection in your life. _he wants to protect me & he will!_

I rely on god to get me through the hard & challenging points of school & life. he has ~~kept~~ lead me to a righteous path for me.

THE SHEPHERD'S CALL

6) **John 13:15** - *"For I gave you an example that you also should do as I did to you."*

From today's scripture, how does **THE** Shepherd inspire **you** to shepherd **your** flock?

let the lord guide me, I want to be someone other people can come to, from K-life I want to not be in relationship because it looks fun & Everyone else has and says I

MINUTE OF MEDITATION _do. I'm not ready_
"For it is You who blesses the righteous man, O Lord, You surround him with favor as with a shield" (Psalm 5:12). _I don't have time to spend!_

PRAYER

Adoration, **C**onfession, **T**hanksgiving, **S**upplication

The Return of the Lost Sheep

"It was for freedom that Christ set us free; therefore keep standing firm and do not be subject again to a yoke of slavery" (Galatians 5:1).

Psalm 6

Born in 1820 on a plantation (a slavery compound in Dorchester County, Maryland), Harriet Tubman will forever be praised as the "conductor" of the Underground Railroad who emancipated as many as 300 slaves from lives of terror and bondage to a walk of freedom and humanity. As a 12-year-old, Harriet began her sacrificial love of justice when she witnessed a slave driver about to throw a heavy object at a fellow slave. Harriet stepped in the path of the object and intercepted the throw in her skull, causing a lifetime of headaches and narcolepsy.

She once said, "You'll be free or die. ... I had reasoned this out in my mind; there was one of two things I had a right to, liberty, or death; if I could not have one, I would have the other; for no man should take me alive; I should fight for my liberty as long as my strength lasted, and when the time came for me to go, the Lord would let them take me."

"But now having been freed from sin and enslaved to God, you derive your benefit, resulting in sanctification, and the outcome, eternal life" (Romans 6:22).

1) **Psalm 6:1-7** - *"O Lord, do not rebuke me in Your anger, nor chasten me in Your wrath. Be gracious to me, O Lord, for I am pining away; heal me, O Lord, for my bones are dismayed. And my soul is greatly dismayed; but You, O Lord—how long? Return, O Lord, rescue my soul; save me because of Your lovingkindness. For there is no mention of You in death; in Sheol who will give You thanks? I am weary with my sighing; every night I make my bed swim, I dissolve my couch with my tears. My eye has wasted away with grief; it has become old because of all my adversaries."*

   —> prayer
   Describe the thoughts and feelings of a repentant heart. —> falling on your knees
   freedom, challenges, this is so tempting & really hard right now, this is not what God want me to do, what would Jesus do? does this honor & glorify the Lord

2) **Romans 2:5** - *"But because of your stubbornness and unrepentant heart you are storing up wrath for yourself in the day of wrath and revelation of the righteous judgment of God."*

   1 John 1:9 - *"If we confess our sins, He is faithful and righteous to forgive us our sins and to cleanse us from all unrighteousness."*
   What is the difference between confession and repentance?
   we can confess our sins and be forgiven but we need repentence so we try and prevent that sin from happening over & over again!

3) **Mark 1:15** - *"... and saying, 'The time is fulfilled, and the kingdom of God is at hand; repent and believe in the gospel.'"*

Why is repentance such a powerful experience? → *feels freeing*

Because it feels like you have defeated satan & your on god's path & life for you & what's a better plan than gods!

4) **Acts 3:19** - *"Therefore repent and return, so that your sins may be wiped away, in order that times of refreshing may come from the presence of the Lord."*
→ *trust in the word & look to* → *Repentance: God loves us*
It's hard to truly repent *so much & is so good!*

Describe your personal experience with confession and repentance.

I find that some sins to me are easier to commit & admit to than others because we are all earthly

5) **Psalm 6:8-10** - *"Depart from me, all you who do iniquity, for the Lord has heard the voice of my weeping. The Lord has heard my supplication, the Lord receives my prayer. All my enemies will be ashamed and greatly dismayed; they shall turn back, they will suddenly be ashamed."* *(picture on certain thing?)*

Psalm 119:45 - *"And I will walk at liberty, for I seek Your precepts."*

2 Corinthians 3:17 - *"Now the Lord is the Spirit, and where the Spirit of the Lord is, there is liberty."*

What does it feel like to walk in the safety, forgiveness, and freedom your Shepherd brings?

it feels very confident its awesome its important to go to god & because we want to be more like Jesus. walking w/the word!

6) **Psalm 51:15** - *"O Lord, open my lips, that my mouth may declare your praise."*

What is our appropriate response as God cleanses our repentant hearts? Why?

to be open to that, and allow the lord to work in us & change us, for the better. He is helping us be the

THE SHEPHERD'S CALL best we can be!

7) **John 13:15** - *"For I gave you an example that you also should do as I did to you."*

From today's scripture, how does **THE** Shepherd inspire **you** to shepherd **your** flock?

I want to become more like him & really focus on my words & choices & actions & reflecting the lord.

MINUTE OF MEDITATION
"Return, O Lord, rescue my soul; save me because of Your lovingkindness"
(Psalm 6:4).

PRAYER
Adoration, **C**onfession, **T**hanksgiving, **S**upplication

The Shepherd's Shield

"My shield is with God, who saves the upright in heart" (Psalm 7:10).

Psalm 7

The well-known words of Romans 8:38-39 open a picture window into a room filled with valuable heirlooms and treasures from the pages of scripture antiquity. The featured display is a map to the Shepherd's heart of protection for the lambs in His personally adopted flock of believers:

"For I am convinced that neither death, nor life, nor angels, nor principalities, nor things present, nor things to come, nor powers, nor height, nor depth, nor any other created thing, will be able to separate us from the love of God, which is in Christ Jesus our Lord."

Another window into this hallowed room is provided by the worship song that echoes Scripture when it simply proclaims, "Thou, O Lord, art a shield about me."

1) **2 Samuel 22:3** - *"My God, my rock, in whom I take refuge, my shield and the horn of my salvation, my stronghold and my refuge; my savior, You save me from violence."*

   Genesis 15:1 - *"After these things the word of the Lord came to Abram in a vision, saying, 'Do not fear, Abram, I am a shield to you; your reward shall be very great.'"*

   Picture Jesus standing with the Shepherd's staff on His unshakable, unmovable foundation and the rod of His infinite power. Before Him is His flock, His church, the people of His inheritance. As one of His lambs, continue to picture Satan's army of demons attacking the flock. Describe your dependence on Jesus alone to protect you from the attack.

   He will always protect us trust even when it's hard!
   even though it might not
   be how we expect it! he is so good always trust in him

2) **Ephesians 6:14-16** - *"Stand firm therefore, having girded your loins with truth, and having put on the breastplate of righteousness, and having shod your feet with the preparation of the gospel of peace; in addition to all, taking up the shield of faith with which you will be able to extinguish all the flaming arrows of the evil one."*

   What is the "shield of faith," and how do you use it to protect you?

   trusting in the lord to do & prevent things if in his plan, use your faith to destress and faith to protect my mind & thoughts.

   What makes faith such a powerful weapon?

   Because god is faithful and faith is beyond powerful as you believe in something you can't always physically see!

3) **Proverbs 30:5** - *"Every word of God is tested; He is a shield to those who take refuge in Him."*

→ go to him for guidence / protection

Psalm 18:2 - *"The Lord is my rock and my fortress and my deliverer, my God, my rock, in whom I take refuge; my shield and the horn of my salvation, my stronghold."*

When tempted by Satan with lust, bitterness, pride, or anxiety, you can choose to run toward the Shepherd or toward temptation. How is that going for you personally?

when recently I fell it's been hard but reflecting on that I've relized I'm needing to go to the lord & rely on him more!

4) **John 10:4** - *"When he puts forth all his own, he goes ahead of them, and the sheep follow him because they know his voice."*

stop trying to control everything myself!

Psalm 33:20 - *"Our soul waits for the Lord; He is our help and our shield."*

To follow Jesus is to "wait on the Lord." How do you need to "wait and follow" today?

try to I pray & wait and let the lord guide me! Being patience with what he has planned for my future!

THE SHEPHERD'S CALL

5) **John 13:15** - *"For I gave you an example that you also should do as I did to you."*

From today's scripture, how does **THE** Shepherd inspire **you** to shepherd **your** flock?

encourage prayer & reminding myself that your made in GOD'S image not the image of this world! Being patient & a good listener!

MINUTE OF MEDITATION

"I will give thanks to the Lord according to His righteousness and will sing praise to the name of the Lord Most High" (Psalm 7:17).

PRAYER

Adoration, **C**onfession, **T**hanksgiving, **S**upplication

The Signs of the Shepherd

"Oh, give ear, Shepherd of Israel, You who lead Joseph like a flock; You who are enthroned above the cherubim, shine forth" (Psalm 80:1).

Psalm 8²

Through the reverence of your imagination, hit the pause button of your mind and go on a journey with me. Travel to the ancient Holy Land, and ascend the side of a rugged mountain, halfway between Jerusalem and Jericho in the desolate, arid wilderness of southern Israel. Then, on one of the hillsides, you will notice a small herd of sheep and a faithful shepherd keeping watch over the flock in the late hour of the quiet and peaceful night. As the lambs rest peacefully in one of the rare grassy patches of nutrition and comfort, the shepherd looks up into the autumn sky and beholds the magnitude and majesty of the giant billboard above him. In the vast expanse of stars, planets, and darkness, the shepherd sees the signature of God as the Creator displays His wonder in the sky.

The shepherd begins to sing in amazement, "Oh Lord, our Lord, how majestic is Your name in all the earth, Who have displayed Your splendor above the heavens! God of wonders beyond our galaxy, You are holy, holy. The universe displays Your majesty! You are holy, holy."

1) **The Billboard of God's Name:** Jehovah

   Why does God's name invoke such power, awe, and reverence? *→ deep respect & for someone or something*

   he is the almighty & he is always in control & has our best interest, he is the creator of what we're constantly surrounded by it's breathe taking!

2) **The Billboard of God's Awesome Majesty**

   How does the cosmos display God's greatness?

   he is the creator of the order of the cosmos & the universe only he could do that!

3) **The Billboard of God's Power**

   NASA has proved that the entire cosmos, from its very inception, expanded a billion light years in the first trillionth of a second, affirming the supernatural, indescribable power of God. How does His great power inspire you in your personal battle to defeat the devil's endless temptations in your mind?

   GOD has always been there & he will always be there for you! Don't let yourself think it's impossible because it's not! do your best for the Lord & work & pray to defeat the devil's endless temptations in our minds!

4) The Billboard of God's Brilliance

The DNA molecule in a human cell is, by far, the most brilliant miniature machine ever built, giving the human genome 150 trillion gigabytes of capacity, millions of times more complex than *all* Apple watches combined! Does that display of God's brilliance inspire your heart to worship and praise? Why or why not?

_____

_____

5) The Billboard of God's Love

Isaiah 53:5-6 - *"But He was pierced through for our transgressions, He was crushed for our iniquities; the chastening for our well-being fell upon Him, and by His scourging we are healed. All of us like sheep have gone astray, each of us has turned to his own way; but the Lord has caused the iniquity of us all to fall on Him."*

Philippians 2:5-8 - *"Have this attitude in yourselves which was also in Christ Jesus, who, although He existed in the form of God, did not regard equality with God a thing to be grasped, but emptied Himself, taking the form of a bond-servant, and being made in the likeness of men. Being found in appearance as a man, He humbled Himself by becoming obedient to the point of death, even death on a cross."*

Why did the Shepherd became a lamb like us, taking on human form?

_____

_____

Describe the quality of love and the commitment to love found in the heart of a truly great Shepherd.

_____

_____

6) The Billboard of You!

2 Corinthians 3:2-3 - *"You are our letter, written in our hearts, known and read by all men; being manifested that you are a letter of Christ, cared for by us, written not with ink but with the Spirit of the living God, not on tablets of stone but on tablets of human hearts."*
How can you be God's letter, or billboard, today?

_____

_____

How might you need to redesign your billboard so that others will be drawn to the Shepherd whose nourishment and protection they need?

_____

_____

THE SHEPHERD'S CALL

7) **John 13:15** - *"For I gave you an example that you also should do as I did to you."*

From today's scripture, how does **THE** Shepherd inspire **you** to shepherd **your** flock?

_____

_____

MINUTE OF MEDITATION

"O Lord, our Lord, how majestic is Your name in all the earth, Who have displayed Your splendor above the heavens" (Psalm 8:1).

PRAYER

Adoration, Confession, Thanksgiving, Supplication

Trust

"The Lord also will be a stronghold for the oppressed, a stronghold in times of trouble; and those who know Your name will put their trust in You, for You, O Lord, have not forsaken those who seek You" (Psalm 9:9-10).

Psalm 9

I hired the defensive coordinator of my college football team to come to Missouri and help me run our summer sports camp just after I graduated. I was so young and inexperienced. I knew he could bring some much-needed wisdom and discipline to our staff. Coach Utley was the toughest coach I'd ever met, but he was loved by our team for his contagious personality and his caring heart for the players on his defensive front.

During staff training week that summer, Coach Utley and his seven-year-old son, Lee, were in our small ski boat pulling a large football player on a slalom ski behind the boat. When the skier cut hard from one side of the wake to the other, something happened that I've never seen before or since that fateful day.

The boat flipped upside down, throwing Coach and the driver overboard. Coach Utley quickly realized Lee was not with him, so he began to swim frantically around the boat, crying out Lee's name. There was no answer. Lee had apparently disappeared into the deep water below. In a last-ditch effort to find his son, Coach ducked under the capsized boat "turtled" on the surface and popped up in the air pocket created by the sides. Miraculously, Lee was treading water in that air pocket, waiting for his daddy to find him.

The reunion was exhilarating, to say the least. Hugs, tears, and words of joy and affection were exchanged. Coach then swam Lee to the shore in grateful silence. As the reunited father-son pair walked up the hill to their cabin, Coach cradled Lee affectionately in his arms.

After a few minutes, Coach asked Lee, "Son, were you scared?"

Lee returned a warm smile and said, "I knew you'd be there, Daddy."

"I knew you'd be there, Daddy" --faith in its purest form from the lips of a seven-year-old.

1) **Proverbs 3:5-6** - *"Trust in the Lord with all your heart and do not lean on your own understanding. In all your ways acknowledge Him, and He will make your paths straight."*

How will *completely* trusting the Shepherd for their protection, well-being, and needs keep the lambs from getting lost and harmed?

_____

_____

So what makes Jesus, your Shepherd, completely trustworthy?

_____

_____

... in your needs for pleasure?

_____

_____

... in your future plans?

_____

_____

... in your needs for intimacy?

_____

_____

If you truly trust Jesus, how will it affect your response to temptation and tendency to wander from the flock?

_____

_____

2) **Jeremiah 17:7-8** - *"Blessed is the man who trusts in the Lord and whose trust is the Lord. For he will be like a tree planted by the water, that extends its roots by a stream and will not fear when the heat comes; but its leaves will be green, and it will not be anxious in a year of drought nor cease to yield fruit."*

What is God's promise to the lamb who trusts in the Shepherd?

_____

_____

3) **Isaiah 43:2** - *"When you pass through the waters, I will be with you; and through the rivers, they will not overflow you. When you walk through the fire, you will not be scorched, nor will the flame burn you."*

To what extent can you trust the Shepherd?

_____

_____

To what extent *will* you trust the Shepherd? Why?

_____

_____

4) **Proverbs 30:5** - *"Every word of God is tested; He is a shield to those who take refuge in Him."*

   Ephesians 6:16 - *"In addition to all, taking up the shield of faith with which you will be able to extinguish all the flaming arrows of the evil one."*

   Psalm 115:9 - *"O Israel, trust in the Lord; He is their help and their shield."*

   What are the flaming arrows of the enemy, and how might the protective shield of your Shepherd help you?

   _____

   _____

THE SHEPHERD'S CALL

5) **John 13:15** - *"For I gave you an example that you also should do as I did to you."*

   From today's scripture, how does **THE** Shepherd inspire **you** to shepherd **your** flock?

   _____

   _____

MINUTE OF MEDITATION

"I will give thanks to the Lord with all my heart; I will tell of all Your wonders. I will be glad and exult in You; I will sing praise to Your name, O Most High" (Psalm 9:1-2).

PRAYER

Adoration, **C**onfession, **T**hanksgiving, **S**upplication

The Righteousness of the Lamb

"For the Lord is righteous, He loves righteousness; the upright will behold His face" (Psalm 11:7).

Psalm 11

For 3,500 years, the Hebrew nation sacrificed only unblemished lambs on the day of Passover celebration. Is it any wonder that when *the Lamb* was being sacrificed for the sins of all mankind, He too would be found "not guilty" and worthy of the ultimate sacrifice for our salvation?

In Exodus 12:5, God speaks to Moses as he prepares for the last of the ten plagues that would convince the pharaoh of Egypt to set God's people free from 400 years of bondage. God's instructions are well known throughout all Judaism and the Christian faith. For God to grant mercy to a Hebrew household from an overnight plague that would kill all the firstborn throughout Egypt, each participating Hebrew family would need to sacrifice an *unblemished* lamb and place its blood on the doorposts of the home as a sign that the family had faith in His command to Moses. This Passover night was celebrated by the Hebrew nation each year from that day forward.

The day of Jesus' crucifixion some 3,500 years later was the day before Passover, when the sacrificial lambs were being examined by the high priest. It was no coincidence that as the lambs were being proclaimed "unblemished" by the high priest, the one true sacrificial Lamb was being examined by Pontius Pilate. It was then, after examining Jesus, that Pilate publicly proclaimed in John 19:4, *"Behold, I am bringing Him out to you so that you may know that I find no guilt in Him."*

1) **Jeremiah 23:6** - *"In His days Judah will be saved, and Israel will dwell securely; and this is His name by which He will be called, 'The Lord our righteousness.'"*

   Define *righteousness* as it relates to God. Give at least three synonyms for *righteousness* as each one describes His attributes.

   _____

   _____

2) **Proverbs 12:28** - *"In the way of righteousness is life, and in its pathway there is no death."*

   How does the righteousness of God make the path for His lambs to follow exceedingly clear?

   _____

   _____

   How does the righteousness of God inspire you to cling closely to His side?

   _____

   _____

3) **2 Corinthians 5:21** - *"He made Him who knew no sin to be sin on our behalf, so that we might become the righteousness of God in Him."*

How is the righteousness of God imputed to a believer (i.e., our sin exchanged for His righteousness; His righteousness for our sin)?

_____

_____

4) **Romans 4:3** - *"For what does the Scripture say? 'Abraham believed God, and it was credited to him as righteousness.'"*

What role does our faith play in receiving the gift of God's righteousness?

_____

_____

5) **Romans 1:17** - *"For in it the righteousness of God is revealed from faith to faith; as it is written, 'But the righteous man shall live by faith.'"*

How does faith enable us to walk in the righteousness of God?

_____

_____

THE SHEPHERD'S CALL

6) **John 13:15** - *"For I gave you an example that you also should do as I did to you."*

From today's scripture, how does **THE** Shepherd inspire **you** to shepherd **your** flock?

_____

_____

MINUTE OF MEDITATION
"For the Lord is righteous, He loves righteousness; the upright will behold His face" (Psalm 11:7).

PRAYER
Adoration, **C**onfession, **T**hanksgiving, **S**upplication

<u>Dependence upon the Shepherd</u>

"The Lord has looked down from heaven upon the sons of men to see if there are any who understand, who seek after God. They have all turned aside, together they have become corrupt; there is no one who does good, not even one" (Psalm 14:2-3).

Psalm 14

Until He becomes your all-in-all, He is really your nothing at all.

Looking back at my football days as both a player and a coach, I'm bewildered by the quality of our shepherds and the lack of commitment by the flock. Hayden Fry was our shepherd at SMU football. He was a *really* good coach; he was good to his players and as innovative as it gets. Approximately 10 percent of his players "gave it all" on and off the field; 90 percent strayed from the shepherd's call at night, on weekends, and out of season.

The picture was similar at Texas A&M in my short tenure as a coach. Our shepherd was Gene Stallings. Like Coach Fry, he was one of the very best and eventually won a national championship at Alabama. Even though both coaches were greatly loved and admired by players, coaches, and fans, both teams could have done better if the coaches and players had completely pursued their shepherd's lead. Both teams lost games they should have won to more-faithful flocks. In both cases, the coaches were fired because the sheep were not "all in" as they should have been.

There is no better coach/shepherd than Jesus! God's love story is the best love story we'll ever be invited into. To leave the flock and follow another, less-well-intended shepherd is unthinkable, yet the sheep stray, *"for all have sinned and fall short of the glory of God"* (Romans 3:23).

1) **Luke 15:20-24** - *"So he got up and came to his father. But while he was still a long way off, his father saw him and felt compassion for him, and ran and embraced him and kissed him. And the son said to him, 'Father, I have sinned against heaven and in your sight; I am no longer worthy to be called your son.' But the father said to his slaves, 'Quickly bring out the best robe and put it on him, and put a ring on his hand and sandals on his feet; and bring the fattened calf, kill it, and let us eat and celebrate; for this son of mine was dead and has come to life again; he was lost and has been found.' And they began to celebrate."*

In this story, which may be the most-well-known parable of all time, the incredible patience of the father reflects well the heart of God in His unceasing commitment to the flock He calls His own. Describe the heart of our Shepherd.

_____

_____

2) **Luke 15:4-7** - *"What man among you, if he has a hundred sheep and has lost one of them, does not leave the ninety-nine in the open pasture and go after the one which is lost until he finds it? When he has found it, he lays it on his shoulders, rejoicing. And when he comes home, he calls together his friends and his neighbors, saying to them, 'Rejoice with me, for I have found my sheep which was lost!' I tell you that in the same way, there will be more joy in heaven over one sinner who repents than over ninety-nine righteous persons who need no repentance."*

"Aggressive pursuit": Describe these two action words as they relate to the heart of your Shepherd.

_____

_____

3) **Romans 5:8** - *"But God demonstrates His own love toward us, in that while we were yet sinners, Christ died for us."*

John 10:14 - *"I am the good shepherd, and I know My own and My own know Me."*

When and where did the Shepherd find you when you were the furthest away from His care?

_____

_____

How did He come after you and bring you back safely to His pasture of grace?

_____

_____

4) **Romans 5:17** - *"For if by the transgression of the one, death reigned through the one, much more those who receive the abundance of grace and of the gift of righteousness will reign in life through the One, Jesus Christ."*

What does His "abundance of grace" mean to you today?

_____

_____

5) **Psalm 78:52** - *"But He led forth His own people like sheep and guided them in the wilderness like a flock."*

As you travel in the wilderness of this broken world, how does He guide you?

_____

_____

In what way(s) do you need to walk more closely by His side?

_____

_____

THE SHEPHERD'S CALL

6) **John 13:15** - *"For I gave you an example that you also should do as I did to you."*

From today's scripture, how does **THE** Shepherd inspire **you** to shepherd **your** flock?

_____

_____

MINUTE OF MEDITATION

"For God is with the righteous generation. You would put to shame the counsel of the afflicted, but the Lord is his refuge" (Psalm 14:5b-6).

PRAYER

Adoration, **C**onfession, **T**hanksgiving, **S**upplication

The Contentment of the Lamb

"The Lord is the portion of my inheritance and my cup; You support my lot. The lines have fallen to me in pleasant places; indeed, my heritage is beautiful to me" (Psalm 16:5-6).

Psalm 16

Being a native Texan, I can laugh at the jest about our Texas tendency to dream excessively: "A Texan doesn't want much land ... just everything that adjoins his property."

In a similar satirical manner, Dr. Seuss tells a story about Yertle the Turtle, who wanted to see and own the world by stacking all the turtles in his happy little pond so he could stand on their backs and see the world that he believed he had the right to rule. With little care for the pain he was causing the other turtles, Yertle demanded that all turtles climb on each other's backs to give his self-made throne a worldwide view. That is, until a turtle named Mack, at the bottom of the stack, burped, which caused the entire stack to come tumbling down and plummeted Yertle the Turtle to the floor of the muddy pond below.

1) **Psalm 16:1-2** - *"Preserve me, O God, for I take refuge in You. I said to the Lord, 'You are my Lord; I have no good besides You.'"*

   What might it mean to say, "I have no good besides You"?
   _____
   _____

2) **Philippians 4:11-12** - *"Not that I speak from want, for I have learned to be content in whatever circumstances I am. I know how to get along with humble means, and I also know how to live in prosperity; in any and every circumstance I have learned the secret of being filled and going hungry, both of having abundance and suffering need."*

   Like Yertle the Turtle and Texans in the satires, what are the dangers of greed?
   _____
   _____

   Describe the virtue of contentment experienced by a lamb who "grazes in the pasture" of Jesus our Shepherd?
   _____
   _____

3) **Psalm 23:1** - *"The Lord is my Shepherd, I shall not want."*

   If Jesus is your Shepherd, is He enough to you? In what ways?
   _____
   _____

Why should Jesus' provision of grace be sufficient for you?

_____

_____

Honestly describe how your heart seeks after more, even when you already have Jesus' provision granted to you.

_____

_____

4) **Philippians 4:5-7** - *"Let your gentle spirit be known to all men. The Lord is near. Be anxious for nothing, but in everything by prayer and supplication with thanksgiving let your requests be made known to God. And the peace of God, which surpasses all comprehension, will guard your hearts and your minds in Christ Jesus."*

How does greed lead to anxiety?

_____

_____

5) **Psalm 16:11** - *"You will make known to me the path of life; in Your presence is fullness of joy; in Your right hand there are pleasures forever."*

What is David trying to tell you in this passage?

_____

_____

How would your life be different if Jesus were truly enough for you?

_____

_____

THE SHEPHERD'S CALL

6) **John 13:15** - *"For I gave you an example that you also should do as I did to you."*

From today's scripture, how does **THE** Shepherd inspire **you** to shepherd **your** flock?

_____

_____

MINUTE OF MEDITATION
"You will make known to me the path of life; in Your presence is fullness of joy; in Your right hand there are pleasures forever" (Psalm 16:11).

PRAYER
Adoration, **C**onfession, **T**hanksgiving, **S**upplication

The Shepherd's Delight

"He brought me forth also into a broad place; He rescued me, because He delighted in me" (Psalm 18:19).

Psalm 18

In my cluttered closet where I grab a shirt and pair of jeans and put on my cowboy boots each morning, I have a mirror over my dresser. I look into that mirror as little as possible (to avoid looking at my old, wrinkled, hillbilly face)! But when I brush and dry my hair, I look up and smile as I see the *only* two pictures on my mirror. One is of my daughter Courtney, and the other is of my daughter Jamie! Just two pictures. Those two photographs have been hanging on that mirror for more than 20 years.

That's how it goes with a sentimental old dad like me! There "ain't nuthin" like my kids' pictures and the wonderful memories of the days they were under my fatherly care! I cherish those days like diamonds in the sand.

Just across the skinny closet is a treasure chest hidden behind my unimpressive shirt and coat rack. Inside the chest are my life's treasures—my daughters' first tiny shoes, my son's first size-four football cleats, two tiny plaster casts that my son wore on his crooked feet in his toddler bed, and dozens of handwritten cards and love letters from my four children and 15 grandchildren.

That's a daddy's heart, you see! That's why God says in Romans 8:14-16, *"For all who are being led by the Spirit of God, these are sons of God. For you have not received a spirit of slavery leading to fear again, but you have received a spirit of adoption as sons by which we cry out, 'Abba! Father!' The Spirit Himself testifies with our spirit that we are children of God."*

1) **Psalm 18:1-3** - *"'I love You, O Lord, my strength.' The Lord is my rock and my fortress and my deliverer, my God, my rock, in whom I take refuge; my shield and the horn of my salvation, my stronghold. I call upon the Lord, who is worthy to be praised, and I am saved from my enemies."*

How do God's amazing love and constant care as a benevolent father and shepherd give you security as you, His lamb, "graze upon the grassy pastures of the mountainside"?

_____
_____

2) **Zephaniah 3:17** - *"The Lord your God is in your midst, a victorious warrior. He will exult over you with joy, He will be quiet in His love, He will rejoice over you with shouts of joy."*

What feelings should rise inside us as we behold the inviting heart of love that God offers us, His adopted?

_____
_____

3) **1 John 3:1** - *"See how great a love the Father has bestowed on us, that we would be called children of God; and such we are. For this reason the world does not know us, because it did not know Him."*

Psalm 19:1 - *"The heavens are telling of the glory of God; and their expanse is declaring the work of His hands."*

In all the universe, the world's most-astute cosmologists believe that planet earth is the only place suitable for life as we know it today. It's obvious, as science and Scripture become a congruent sonnet, that God built planet earth as a home for His children to grow up and develop a fondness for their Creator-Dad. How can that knowledge change and mold your life as you move closer and closer to the heart of your Shepherd?

_____

_____

4) **Psalm 19:7-11** - *"The law of the Lord is perfect, restoring the soul; the testimony of the Lord is sure, making wise the simple. The precepts of the Lord are right, rejoicing the heart; the commandment of the Lord is pure, enlightening the eyes. The fear of the Lord is clean, enduring forever; the judgments of the Lord are true; they are righteous altogether. They are more desirable than gold, yes, than much fine gold; sweeter also than honey and the drippings of the honeycomb. Moreover, by them Your servant is warned; in keeping them there is great reward."*

In the past week, how have prayer, scriptural meditation, and faith through your own life challenges drawn you closer to your Shepherd's heart?

_____

_____

5) **Psalm 20:7** - *"Some boast in chariots and some in horses, but we will boast in the name of the Lord, our God."*

How should God's amazing love for you influence what you communicate with your words and your lifestyle? Is He the central focus of all you say and do?

_____

_____

THE SHEPHERD'S CALL

6) **John 13:15** - *"For I gave you an example that you also should do as I did to you."*

From today's scripture, how does **THE** Shepherd inspire **you** to shepherd **your** flock?

_____

_____

MINUTE OF MEDITATION
"Therefore I will give thanks to You among the nations, O Lord, and I will sing praises to Your name" (Psalm 18:49).

PRAYER
Adoration, **C**onfession, **T**hanksgiving, **S**upplication

The Shepherd's Sacrifice

"For dogs have surrounded me; a band of evildoers has encompassed me; they pierced my hands and my feet" (Psalm 22:16).

Psalm 22

Eight hundred years before the cruel and brutal Assyrians and Romans began to sentence men to crucifixion, in which metal nails would be driven into a man's hands and feet to impale him to a cross until he had cried out his exhausting scream of pain and anguish, David prophesied the death of our Shepherd in graphic detail.

Why didn't Jesus come to earth when death was delivered quickly by a firing squad, a guillotine, or a lethal injection? Why the crucifixion and the scourge of the Roman flogging? Why did He have to suffer for so long in such great agony?

If you could stand beside me when I actually build a cross in my "The Cross" presentation on college campuses, in prisons, before football teams, and at men's events around the world; and when I then listen to the truly sad, sad stories of murder, abuse, rape, pornography, and drug and alcohol addictions; and when I experience through those conversations the horror of the effects of sin, you'd understand the severity of our offenses before a holy God and the gigantic price that *had* to be paid by *His Son* for those sins committed.

Isaiah 53:5 gives insight into the necessity of suffering of the Lamb when the prophet declared, *"By His scourging we are healed."*

1) **Psalm 22:1-2 -** *"My God, my God, why have You forsaken me? Far from my deliverance are the words of my groaning. O my God, I cry by day, but You do not answer; and by night, but I have no rest."*

   It's impossible for us to comprehend God the Father turning away from God the Son as Jesus hung on the cross, bearing our sins. But what does the prophetic intensity of Jesus' feelings of loneliness there tell us about the depth of His suffering? Which pain do you think was greater, the physical agony or the separation from the Father? Why?

   _____

   _____

2) **Psalm 22:14-15 -** *"I am poured out like water, and all my bones are out of joint; my heart is like wax; it is melted within me. My strength is dried up like a potsherd, and my tongue cleaves to my jaws; and You lay me in the dust of death."*

   What are your thoughts about the necessity of Jesus' six hours of suffering on the cross?

   _____

   _____

3) **Psalm 22:15-18** - *"For dogs have surrounded me; a band of evildoers has encompassed me; they pierced my hands and my feet. I can count all my bones. They look, they stare at me; they divide my garments among them, and for my clothing they cast lots."*

Luke 23:33 - *"When they came to the place called The Skull, there they crucified Him and the criminals, one on the right and the other on the left."*

In the graphic description of Jesus' day of crucifixion in Psalm 22, written a thousand years before Jesus received the fulfillment of this prophecy, David speaks in empathetic clarity. How does this expression of what Jesus endured affect your appreciation of His sacrifice for you? What does it say about how much He loves you?

_____

_____

4) **Luke 23:44** - *"It was now about the sixth hour, and darkness fell over the whole land until the ninth hour."*

In response to His many hours of suffering, the familiar worship song "How Deep the Father's Love for Us" was written to declare, "It was my sin that held Him there until it was accomplished." How do you personally connect with the lyrics of that insightful hymn?

_____

_____

5) **Psalm 22:22-23** - *"I will tell of Your name to my brethren; in the midst of the assembly I will praise You. You who fear the Lord, praise Him; all you descendants of Jacob, glorify Him, and stand in awe of Him, all you descendants of Israel."*

How can you daily remember to praise Jesus for His suffering on behalf of your healing and forgiveness? Perhaps as you're driving to work or climbing into bed?

_____

_____

THE SHEPHERD'S CALL

6) **John 13:15** - *"For I gave you an example that you also should do as I did to you."*

From today's scripture, how does **THE** Shepherd inspire **you** to shepherd **your** flock?

_____

_____

MINUTE OF MEDITATION
"But You, O Lord, be not far off; O You my help, hasten to my assistance"
(Psalm 22:19).

PRAYER
Adoration, **C**onfession, **T**hanksgiving, **S**upplication

The Lord is My Shepherd

"The Lord is my shepherd, I shall not want. He makes me lie down in green pastures; He leads me beside quiet waters. He restores my soul; He guides me in the paths of righteousness for His name's sake"
(Psalm 23:1-3).

Psalm 23

In perhaps the most-widely-known poem of all time, David combines his childhood background of life as a shepherd and his soulful connection with God, the central focus of his life.

The story goes of a small, private dinner gathering of half a dozen noted actors in Hollywood. One of the actors brought an unknown guest to dinner.

One by one in succession around the table, each actor recited a few lines from one of his most-well-known movie scripts. As each actor finished his lines, a round of polite applause was given. The last actor who brought the guest was not as well known. Since he didn't have any famous movie lines to recall, with little inflection or personality he simply recited the 23rd Psalm. The actors were taken aback by the introduction of Scripture into the conversation.

As he completed his brief recital, his unknown guest paused deeply and began to slowly and deliberately recite the same 23rd Psalm. Tears welled up in his eyes as he carefully delivered each meaningful verse. All the dinner guests could tell that the words came from a place of emotional depth in his heart. When he finished, there was neither applause nor words exchanged. Everyone sat in awe and silence. To him, the psalm was not a recital. It was a personal message that God had impressed upon his heart. After a few short moments, the man who brought the unknown guest whispered tenderly, "I knew the psalm, but you know the Shepherd."

1) ***"The Lord is my shepherd..."*** David writes with an enviable personal connection to the heart of *his* Shepherd. What do the first five words of this psalm mean to you today?

   _____

   _____

2) **Psalm 23:2 -** *"He makes me lie down in green pastures; He leads me beside quiet waters."*

   What does this verse say about God's tender care for you?

   _____

   _____

3) **Psalm 23:3 -** *"He restores my soul; He guides me in the paths of righteousness for His name's sake."*

   How does Jesus restore your soul?

   _____

   _____

How does He guide you in the paths of righteousness?

_____

_____

4) **Psalm 23:4-6** - *"Even though I walk through the valley of the shadow of death, I fear no evil, for You are with me; Your rod and Your staff, they comfort me. You prepare a table before me in the presence of my enemies; You have anointed my head with oil; my cup overflows. Surely goodness and lovingkindness will follow me all the days of my life, and I will dwell in the house of the Lord forever."*

We live in an evil, hurtful world and face the certainty of death someday. How can these words of assurance bring peace in light of those hard realities?

_____

_____

5) **John 16:33** - *"These things I have spoken to you, so that in Me you may have peace. In the world you have tribulation, but take courage; I have overcome the world."*

Describe a difficult circumstance you're facing today and the way your Shepherd is bringing you peace in the midst of that challenge.

_____

_____

6) **John 14:16-17** - *"I will ask the Father, and He will give you another Helper, that He may be with you forever; that is the Spirit of truth, whom the world cannot receive, because it does not see Him or know Him, but you know Him because He abides with you and will be in you."*

What is the Holy Spirit's role in bringing you comfort and bravery in the midst of the hurts, worries, and difficulties you face each day?

_____

_____

THE SHEPHERD'S CALL

7) **John 13:15** - *"For I gave you an example that you also should do as I did to you."*

From today's scripture, how does **THE** Shepherd inspire **you** to shepherd **your** flock?

_____

_____

MINUTE OF MEDITATION
"Even though I walk through the valley of the shadow of death, I fear no evil, for You are with me; Your rod and Your staff, they comfort me" (Psalm 23:4).

PRAYER
Adoration, **C**onfession, **T**hanksgiving, **S**upplication

Following the Shepherd

"When he puts forth all his own, he goes ahead of them, and the sheep follow him because they know his voice" (John 10:4).

Psalm 24

When David asked, *"Who may ascend into the hill of the Lord? And who may stand in His holy place?"* (Psalm 24:3), there's a very good chance he was reflecting on the passage of the Torah, which he had surely memorized, where Moses had climbed Horeb, "the mountain of God," and encountered God in the burning bush. It was here that Moses talked to God. It was here that God spoke to Moses. It was here on the holy mountain where God's voice said to Moses, *"Remove your sandals from your feet, for the place on which you are standing is holy ground"* (Exodus 3:5). Reverence, respect, fear, awe ... you can *feel* the emotions consuming Moses as he heard God's clear and certain voice.

Over three-thousand years later and halfway around the world, we can hardly get our minds around the magnitude of this moment when God spoke to Moses and proclaimed, *"I AM WHO I AM."*

So, God asks you and me today through this psalm of David, "Who can approach God and converse today? Who can hear from God *clearly*? Who can communicate with God and hear His voice without static and interruption?" No sooner did David ask this crucial question than he had answered it himself: *"He who has clean hands and a pure heart, who has not lifted up his soul to falsehood and has not sworn deceitfully"* (Psalm 24:4).

This is holy ground. Come to God in reverence and awe. Keep your hands clean. Keep your mind clean. Keep your heart clean. Keep your vocabulary clean. The Shepherd who gave you His sacrificial blood to make you clean also gave you His Holy Spirit to empower you to follow Him and live that way. The closer a lamb is to his Shepherd, the easier it is to follow Him.

1) **1 John 2:1-6** - *"My little children, I am writing these things to you so that you may not sin. And if anyone sins, we have an Advocate with the Father, Jesus Christ the righteous; and He Himself is the propitiation for our sins; and not for ours only, but also for those of the whole world. By this we know that we have come to know Him, if we keep His commandments. The one who says, 'I have come to know Him,' and does not keep His commandments, is a liar, and the truth is not in him; but whoever keeps His word, in him the love of God has truly been perfected. By this we know that we are in Him: the one who says he abides in Him ought himself to walk in the same manner as He walked."*

What part of our purity quest does God take responsibility for?

_____

_____

What part of the purity quest does God ask us to be responsible for?

_____

_____

2) **Matthew 5:8** - *"Blessed are the pure in heart, for they shall see God."*

What is the reward for a life devoted to purity? What does it mean to "see" God?

_____

_____

3) **Revelation 3:20** - *"Behold, I stand at the door and knock; if anyone hears My voice and opens the door, I will come in to him and will dine with him, and he with Me."*

What does it mean to dine with Jesus and have fellowship with Him?

_____

_____

4) Why are "clean hands and a pure heart" essential in this conversation?

_____

_____

5) **John 16:13** - *"But when He, the Spirit of truth, comes, He will guide you into all the truth; for He will not speak on His own initiative, but whatever He hears, He will speak; and He will disclose to you what is to come."*

Acts 1:8a - *"But you will receive power when the Holy Spirit has come upon you."*

What is the Holy Spirit's role in our conversation with God?

_____

_____

6) **Psalm 24:9-10** - *"Lift up your heads, O gates, and lift them up, O ancient doors, that the King of glory may come in! Who is this King of glory? The Lord of hosts, He is the King of glory."*

What is God telling you in this passage?

_____

_____

THE SHEPHERD'S CALL

7) **John 13:15** - *"For I gave you an example that you also should do as I did to you."*

From today's scripture, how does **THE** Shepherd inspire **you** to shepherd **your** flock?

_____

_____

MINUTE OF MEDITATION
"Who is the King of glory? The Lord strong and mighty, the Lord mighty in battle" (Psalm 24:8).

PRAYER
Adoration, **C**onfession, **T**hanksgiving, **S**upplication

The Pathway of the Shepherd

"Make me know Your ways, O Lord; teach me Your paths. Lead me in Your truth and teach me, for You are the God of my salvation; for You I wait all the day" (Psalm 25:4-5).

Psalm 25

When I was a small child, my family raised two sheep. One was jet black, and the other was pure white. We called the black sheep Bonnie and the white sheep Sugar. They were beautiful, sweet, friendly and ... *not* famous for their thinking skills. But I loved those sheep, and as long as we took care of everything for them, they survived and flourished. I never guided sheep on a mountainside journey, but I learned enough about them as a child to be certain that, without a guide, they could never survive.

As God's sheep grazing in earth's vast pastures, where would we be without God's Word to guide us?

In our study today, let's examine some of the Bible's insightful treasures and see why this marvelous book has forever been known as God's book of wisdom.

Abraham Lincoln said, "I believe the Bible is the best gift God has ever given to man." Charles Dickens said the New Testament "is the very best book that ever was or ever will be known in the world." Patrick Henry said, "The Bible is worth all the other books which have ever been printed."

Imagine one book written over a time span of *1,500 years,* with 66 books penned by 40 different writers--from farmers to peasants to fishermen to kings--from three continents, telling one continuous, congruent story from the first word in Genesis to the last word in Revelation--as if one person had written the entire book in one sitting! That's the nature of the Bible we have in our possession today.

It is estimated that the Bible has been printed in somewhere between 4 and 7 billion copies--more than the next top 50 books combined. The Bible has been printed in more than 2,400 languages. (The Koran has only been printed in 114 languages.) In libraries today, there are more than 25,000 early New Testament manuscripts, exact replicas of the New Testaments that date back to as early as AD 45; this far exceeds the combined number of top 50 classic literature books!

1) **Psalm 25:9** - *"He leads the humble in justice, and He teaches the humble His way."*

   What makes a "humble heart" more receptive to God's word of wisdom?

   _____

   _____

   Describe the position of your heart as it relates to your personal study of God's Word.

   _____

   _____

When the heart is proud, what happens when it's exposed to God's Word?

_____

_____

2) **Psalm 25:12** - *"Who is the man who fears the Lord? He will instruct him in the way he should choose."*

What does the "fear of the Lord" have to do with understanding God's guiding Word?

_____

_____

3) **Psalm 25:15-17** - *"My eyes are continually toward the Lord, for He will pluck my feet out of the net. Turn to me and be gracious to me, for I am lonely and afflicted. The troubles of my heart are enlarged; bring me out of my distresses."*

Describe how following the Shepherd's instruction book has guided you through some of your life's most-troubled waters.

_____

_____

4) **Psalm 25:21** - *"Let integrity and uprightness preserve me, for I wait for You."*

Psalm 26:11 - *"But as for me, I shall walk in my integrity; redeem me, and be gracious to me."*

Why is absolute integrity essential in understanding the guidance of the Shepherd through His Word?

_____

_____

Describe one way you need to grow in your personal integrity.

_____

_____

THE SHEPHERD'S CALL

5) **John 13:15** - *"For I gave you an example that you also should do as I did to you."*

From today's scripture, how does **THE** Shepherd inspire **you** to shepherd **your** flock?

_____

_____

MINUTE OF MEDITATION
"To You, O Lord, I lift up my soul. O my God, in You I trust" (Psalm 25:1-2a).

PRAYER
Adoration, Confession, Thanksgiving, Supplication

Fearlessness through Intimacy with the Shepherd

"The Lord is my light and my salvation; whom shall I fear?" (Psalm 27:1).

Psalm 27

The book *Fearless* is a tear-jerking, true story about a U.S. Navy SEAL named Adam Brown who gave his life in the fight to free the world from tyrannical Taliban terrorists in eastern Afghanistan.

This *New York Times* bestseller brilliantly describes Adam's road to SEAL Team Six qualification and his personal battle to overcome cocaine addiction and become one of the truly greatest freedom fighters in U.S. military history.

In spite of losing an eye and the use of one thumb, Adam used fearless perseverance and determination to carry him through battle after battle in training, as well as in combat, to maintain the highest standard of excellence in all he accomplished.

If you mention the name Adam Brown to any Navy SEAL, you will see the utmost respect deeply embedded in his eyes and heart.

The title of the book says it all; *Fearless* was Adam's trademark. He learned how to be a team player from his tightly woven teammates in SEAL Team Six. That team would unquestionably lay down their lives for each other in a split second.

Adam learned how to love his two children, Nathan and Savannah, from his loyal wife, Kelley.

But Adam learned his fearlessness from His Lord and Savior, Jesus Christ. If Adam were alive today, he'd tell you that Jesus' example of His fearless walk up "the hill of the skull" with the cross carried on His torture-shredded back was his (Adam's) road map to courage. *"The Lord is on my side; I will not fear"* (Psalm 118:6, ESV).

1) **Psalm 27:1-2** - *"The Lord is my light and my salvation; whom shall I fear? The Lord is the defense of my life; whom shall I dread? When evildoers came upon me to devour my flesh, my adversaries and my enemies, they stumbled and fell."*

What is the connection between fearlessness and the closeness of your relationship with your Shepherd?

_____

_____

2) **Psalm 27:2-3** - *"When evildoers came upon me to devour my flesh, my adversaries and my enemies, they stumbled and fell. Though a host encamp against me, my heart will not fear; though war arise against me, in spite of this I shall be confident."*

If you use the metaphor of the Shepherd and His flock, where would you, as a lamb, position yourself in the herd if a predator approached?

_____

_____

How does that apply to the way you walk with Jesus?

_____

_____

How do you accomplish that on a daily basis?

_____

_____

3) **Psalm 27:4** - *"One thing I have asked from the Lord, that I shall seek: That I may dwell in the house of the Lord all the days of my life, to behold the beauty of the Lord and to meditate in His temple."*

How do you identify with David in this passage? What do you think heaven will be like?

_____

_____

4) **Psalm 27:5-6** - *"For in the day of trouble He will conceal me in His tabernacle; in the secret place of His tent He will hide me; He will lift me up on a rock. And now my head will be lifted up above my enemies around me, and I will offer in His tent sacrifices with shouts of joy; I will sing, yes, I will sing praises to the Lord."*

To what extent does the mindset of David in this passage strengthen your confidence to walk in fearlessness? Why?

_____

_____

5) **Psalm 27:8** - *"When you said, 'Seek my face,' my heart said to You, 'Your face, O Lord, I shall seek.'"*

How can walking "face to face with Jesus" help you in the battles you face?

_____

_____

THE SHEPHERD'S CALL

6) **John 13:15** - *"For I gave you an example that you also should do as I did to you."*

From today's scripture, how does **THE** Shepherd inspire **you** to shepherd **your** flock?

_____

_____

MINUTE OF MEDITATION

"Wait for the Lord; be strong and let your heart take courage; yes, wait for the Lord" (Psalm 27:14).

PRAYER

Adoration, **C**onfession, **T**hanksgiving, **S**upplication

The Rod of the Shepherd

"For His anger is but for a moment, His favor is for a lifetime; weeping may last for the night, but a shout of joy comes in the morning" (Psalm 30:5).

"The Lord is my strength and my shield" (Psalm 28:7a).

Psalm 30

I once read two interesting viewpoints from two different experienced shepherds. They said the rod of the shepherd serves two purposes, both of which are for the protection of the flock. The rod can be used to strike a predator in pursuit of the flock, and it can be used to discipline a wayward lamb. If a lamb is consistently strong-willed and leaves the herd, repeatedly placing its life in danger, the rod has occasionally been used to strike the leg of the sheep to crack the bone. After the bone is broken, the shepherd carefully splints the leg and, with great love, carefully wraps the splint with soft strips of cloth to keep the splint tight to the tender bone and fastened securely. A shepherd knows that from that day forward, the disciplined lamb will be the closest lamb to his heart and the one that will never leave his side for the rest of its life.

1) **Psalm 30:1-3 -** *"I will extol You, O Lord, for You have lifted me up, and have not let my enemies rejoice over me. O Lord my God, I cried to You for help, and You healed me. O Lord, You have brought up my soul from Sheol; You have kept me alive, that I would not go down to the pit."*

   Psalm 23:4b - *"For You are with me; Your rod and Your staff, they comfort me."*

   Describe a time in your life when the discipline of the Lord became real to you.

   _____

   _____

   How did God use that discipline to bring you back to the safety of His guidance and the protection of the flock?

   _____

   _____

2) **Psalm 30:11-12** - *"You have turned for me my mourning into dancing; You have loosed my sackcloth and girded me with gladness, that my soul may sing praise to You and not be silent. O Lord my God, I will give thanks to You forever."*

In the book *Hinds' Feet on High Places*, author Hannah Hurnard said that God used two "helpers" to keep her two back feet firmly planted so they wouldn't slip as they climbed to higher places that mattered most in life. One was sadness, the other sorrow. Describe how God's "rod of discipline" brings joy to your life through the pain and sadness of the process.

_____

_____

What trials/discipline are you experiencing now, and how can you be joyful in the process?

_____

_____

3) **James 1:1-2** - *"James, a bond-servant of God and of the Lord Jesus Christ, to the twelve tribes who are dispersed abroad: Greetings. Consider it all joy, my brethren, when you encounter various trials."*

How have trials and God's "rod of discipline" given your life the quality of endurance?

_____

_____

4) **Romans 5:3-5** - *"And not only this, but we also exult in our tribulations, knowing that tribulation brings about perseverance; and perseverance, proven character; and proven character, hope; and hope does not disappoint, because the love of God has been poured out within our hearts through the Holy Spirit who was given to us."*

This profound passage of Scripture points out that, like an automatic transmission, tribulations shift gifts into character and character into hope. How has that been true in your life?

_____

_____

5) **Psalm 28:7** - *"The Lord is my strength and my shield; my heart trusts in Him, and I am helped; therefore my heart exults, and with my song I shall thank Him."*

How can this passage strengthen you in your times of trial?

_____

_____

6) **Psalm 31:2, 7** - *"Incline Your ear to me, rescue me quickly; be to me a rock of strength, a stronghold to save me.... I will rejoice and be glad in Your lovingkindness, because You have seen my affliction; You have known the troubles of my soul."*

How have you experienced God's deliverance?

_____

_____

Describe what this passage means to you personally.

_____

_____

THE SHEPHERD'S CALL

7) **John 13:15** - "For I gave you an example that you also should do as I did to you."

From today's scripture, how does **THE** Shepherd inspire you to shepherd **your** flock?

_____

_____

MINUTE OF MEDITATION

"For His anger is but for a moment, His favor is for a lifetime; weeping may last for the night, but a shout of joy comes in the morning" (Psalm 30:5).

PRAYER

Adoration, **C**onfession, **T**hanksgiving, **S**upplication

From Famine to Grassy Hillsides

"How blessed is he whose transgression is forgiven, whose sin is covered! How blessed is the man to whom the Lord does not impute iniquity, and in whose spirit there is no deceit" (Psalm 32:1-2).

Psalm 32

Even though it's been more than 30 years, I'll never forget the week when I saw God in the most tender and pleasant light I believe I've ever seen Him in. My second daughter, Courtney, must have been in second or third grade and came home in tears over a difficult math test. Apparently, the teacher had insisted that in order to go on to the next level, each student had to complete 30 math problems in a minute or two. The hands of the timer moved too swiftly for Courtney's young mind to capture the answers. I recalled all the times I had struggled with testing and came to Courtney's side with as much daddy love as I could give. She let me sit next to her on her bed and go over the problems again and again and again, so she could roll them off her tongue in a breath.

The next day, I walked into the room and saw that beautiful child sitting at her desk with a timer and a stack of practice tests that she had run on the copier after she returned home from another bad day at school. There were five or six tests wadded up and thrown on the floor. Her face was streaked with tears. I could tell in an instant that she had failed again. As I entered, she looked at me and said abruptly, "Get out of my room!" I turned, a little brokenhearted, to walk away. Yeah, I was hurt because she snapped at me and didn't want my help, but mostly I was hurt because her heart was obviously so severely broken.

That night, as I walked into my bedroom to get ready for sleep, I noticed a note on my bed from Courtney. The note read, "Dear Dad, I'm sorry about my adatood. I love you, you're the best." Attached to the note was a little purple sucker. I knew in an instant what she was trying to say: "This purple sucker isn't much, but it's all I've got to tell you how much I love you."

I'll never forget that purple sucker or the fact that I had been memorizing Psalm 103 that week. The part in the passage that had stuck out in my mind was verse 13: *"Just as a father has compassion on his children, so the Lord has compassion on those who fear Him."* That night I understood what the Lord was saying. I wasn't mad at my daughter. I wasn't upset with her. The fact that she had asked me to leave her room and had spoken to me the way she had did not cause me to think any less of her. If that's the way God feels about us when we make a mistake, then I'm a blessed man to receive His grace for all the mistakes I make. Perhaps all He's asking for is a purple sucker.

1) **Psalm 32:3-4** - *"When I kept silent about my sin, my body wasted away through my groaning all day long. For day and night Your hand was heavy upon me; my vitality was drained away as with the fever heat of summer."*

   What is it about sin that drives the Shepherd's lambs into darkness and spiritual famine?

   _____

   _____

2) **John 8:34** - *"Jesus answered them, 'Truly, truly, I say to you, everyone who commits sin is the slave of sin.'"*

   Isaiah 53:6a - *"All of us like sheep have gone astray."*

   When one of Jesus' lambs gets outside the safety of the flock, it can get captured by a predator, stuck on a precipitous hillside, or lost permanently. How does sin endanger a stray sheep in God's flock?

   _____

   _____

3) **Psalm 32:5** - *"I acknowledged my sin to You, and my iniquity I did not hide; I said, 'I will confess my transgressions to the Lord'; and You forgave the guilt of my sin."*

   Why is confessing our sins before the Lord so important?

   _____

   _____

   What does God mean when He says He forgives the "guilt" of our sin?

   _____

   _____

   What do you need to confess to Him today?

   _____

   _____

4) **Psalm 103:10-13** - *"He has not dealt with us according to our sins, nor rewarded us according to our iniquities. For as high as the heavens are above the earth, so great is His lovingkindness toward those who fear Him. As far as the east is from the west, so far has He removed our transgressions from us. Just as a father has compassion on his children, so the Lord has compassion on those who fear Him."*

   What is the Good Shepherd trying to tell you today about the power and availability of His forgiveness?

   _____

   _____

THE SHEPHERD'S CALL

5) **John 13:15** - *"For I gave you an example that you also should do as I did to you."*

From today's scripture, how does **THE** Shepherd inspire **you** to shepherd **your** flock?

_____

_____

MINUTE OF MEDITATION

"How blessed is he whose transgression is forgiven, whose sin is covered"
(Psalm 32:1).

PRAYER

Adoration, **C**onfession, **T**hanksgiving, **S**upplication

The Fear of God

"Let all the earth fear the Lord; let all the inhabitants of the world stand in awe of Him" (Psalm 33:8).

Psalm 33

The flock in the care of the Good Shepherd has nothing to fear but the fear of the Shepherd Himself. The perspectives of some wonderful sources on "the fear of God" are insightful. Even Wikipedia provides worthy insight. (Imagine that!)

Wikipedia: *"There are two kinds of fear: lower fear is the fear of punishment, higher fear is divine awe and glory."*

John Piper: *"The fear of God is when He is in your mind and heart so powerful, so awesome, so holy, that you would not dare to run away from Him but only run to Him."*

Luke 1:50: *"And His mercy is upon generation after generation toward those who fear Him."*

Psalm 111:10a: *"The fear of the Lord is the beginning of wisdom."*

Proverbs 23:17: *"Do not let your heart envy sinners, but live in the fear of the Lord always."*

Pope Francis: *"The fear of God is a joyful awareness of God's grandeur."*

Psalm 56:11: *"In God I have put my trust, I shall not be afraid. What can man do to me?"*

1 John 4:18: *"There is no fear in love; but perfect love casts out fear, because fear involves punishment, and the one who fears is not perfected in love."*

Augustine: *"The fear of the Lord is the crown of wisdom."*

Dietrich Bonhoeffer: *"This is the first commandment, the entire gospel: Fear God, instead of the many things you fear."*

Billy Graham: *"To fear God is to have a deep reverence for Him and to stand in awe of His holiness and majesty and power and love."*

Oswald Chambers: *"When you fear God, you fear nothing else. When you do not fear God, you fear everything else."*

Charles Spurgeon: *"He who fears God has nothing else to fear."*

Benjamin Franklin: *"Fear God so your enemies will fear you."*

1) **Psalm 128:1-4** - *"How blessed is everyone who fears the Lord, who walks in His ways. When you shall eat of the fruit of your hands, you will be happy and it will be well with you. Your wife shall be like a fruitful vine within your house, your children like olive plants around your table. Behold, for thus shall the man be blessed who fears the Lord."*

   This amazing passage promises four of the most-fulfilling things a man can ever hope for if he spends his life in the fear of the Lord. Describe each one and what it means:

   a. You shall eat the fruit of your hands.

   _____

   b. You'll be happy, and it will go well with you.

   _____

   c. Your wife will be a fruitful vineyard. (Godly children/the fruit of the Spirit) _____

   d. Your children will be like olive plants (oil of gladness)

   _____

2) **Psalm 33:1-3** - *"Sing for joy in the Lord, O you righteous ones; praise is becoming to the upright. Give thanks to the Lord with the lyre; Sing praises to Him with a harp of ten strings. Sing to Him a new song; play skillfully with a shout of joy."*

   Why does the fear of the Lord produce a life of promise and thanksgiving?

   _____
   _____

   How does that truth speak to you personally today?

   _____
   _____

3) **Psalm 37:4, 6, 9** - *"Delight yourself in the Lord; and He will give you the desires of your heart. ... He will bring forth your righteousness as the light and your judgment as the noonday. ... For evildoers will be cut off, but those who wait for the Lord, they will inherit the land."*

   How and why does the Word of the Lord fill you with the fear of the Lord?

   _____
   _____

4) **Psalm 33:10-11** - *"The Lord nullifies the counsel of the nations; He frustrates the plans of the peoples. The counsel of the Lord stands forever, the plans of His heart from generation to generation."*
What is God saying to you in this passage?

_____

_____

How does this truth shape the way you approach your goals, dreams, and daily activities?

_____

_____

5) **Psalm 33:16-17, 20-21** - *"The king is not saved by a mighty army; a warrior is not delivered by great strength. A horse is a false hope for victory; nor does it deliver anyone by its great strength. ... Our soul waits for the Lord; He is our help and our shield. For our heart rejoices in Him, because we trust in His holy name."*

From where do your victories come? _____

Who is your strength? _____

Who fights your battles? _____

What does this say to your personal pride?

_____

_____

Who gets the credit for what you accomplish?

_____

6) **John 10:12-14** - *"He who is a hired hand, and not a shepherd, who is not the owner of the sheep, sees the wolf coming, and leaves the sheep and flees, and the wolf snatches them and scatters them. He flees because he is a hired hand and is not concerned about the sheep. I am the good shepherd, and I know My own and My own know Me."*
How does the fear of the Lord eradicate the fear of the things of the world, the flesh, and the devil?

_____

_____

THE SHEPHERD'S CALL
7) **John 13:15** - *"For I gave you an example that you also should do as I did to you."*

From today's scripture, how does **THE** Shepherd inspire **you** to shepherd **your** flock?

_____

_____

MINUTE OF MEDITATION

"And His mercy is upon generation after generation toward those who fear Him" (Luke 1:50).

PRAYER

Adoration, Confession, Thanksgiving, Supplication

The Shepherd's Healing Touch

"The righteous cry, and the Lord hears and delivers them out of all their troubles. The Lord is near to the brokenhearted and saves those who are crushed in spirit" (Psalm 34:17-18).

Psalm 34

I was diagnosed with leukemia in the summer of 2000. My oncologist told me I had very little chance of survival and only promised me nine months to go home and "get your house in order." If I did survive, I was told, I would never be the same.

That was tough news for a happily married man and father of four who anticipated countless days ahead of happiness leading folks to Christ. But God had a perfect plan. As Jeremiah 29:11 says, *"'For I know the plans that I have for you,' declares the Lord, 'plans for welfare and not for calamity to give you a future and a hope.'"*

God has given miraculous wisdom to a team of macromolecular doctors at Washington State University--the wisdom to find the DNA anomaly in my genetic code and miraculously treat that microscopic DNA particle in every cell in my bone marrow with a non-toxic daily pill. Yes, it was a miracle drug. Six weeks later, my blood was normal and remains so today.

No, God doesn't heal everyone immediately, but He heals every day in ways we see and in ways we don't. As I pray with hurting people, I see God healing emotional and spiritual pain. I watch Him heal abuse, rape, hatred, abandonment, sudden loss of loved ones, addictions, self-hatred, and a host of other emotional diseases on a regular basis. God is definitely a healing God. A good shepherd of a flock is continuously looking out for hurting sheep and ready to come to the rescue with a splint or a bandage. That's what good shepherds do.

1) **Psalm 34:19** - *"Many are the afflictions of the righteous, but the Lord delivers him out of them all."*

   How has God healed you in profound ways in your times of physical, spiritual, and emotional need?

   _____

   _____

2) **1 Peter 5:10** - *"After you have suffered for a little while, the God of all grace, who called you to His eternal glory in Christ, will Himself perfect, confirm, strengthen and establish you."*

   Describe God's heart for restoring His wounded sheep.

   _____

   _____

3) **Psalm 40:1-3** - *"I waited patiently for the Lord; and He inclined to me and heard my cry. He brought me up out of the pit of destruction, out of the miry clay, and He set my feet upon a rock making my footsteps firm. He put a new song in my mouth, a song of praise to our God; many will see and fear and will trust in the Lord."*

Describe the experience and joy of God's healing touch in your life.

_____

_____

4) **2 Corinthians 4:15** - *"For all things are for your sakes, so that the grace which is spreading to more and more people may cause the giving of thanks to abound to the glory of God."*

What is our proper response to the way God is constantly healing us? How consistent are you at being thankful?

_____

_____

5) **Ephesians 2:10** - *"For we are His workmanship, created in Christ Jesus for good works, which God prepared beforehand so that we would walk in them."*

The Greek word for *workmanship* is *poiema*. In a sense, you are God's poem. Just like life, poetry doesn't always rhyme; but that's because you're not to the end of the stanza. The rhyme is coming if you're patient and keep reading. Describe a time where your life didn't "rhyme," and you wondered where God was. Then what happened when the rhyme came?

_____

_____

Why did God save the rhyme for His perfect timing?

_____

_____

6) **Psalm 103:3** - *"Who pardons all your iniquities, who heals all your diseases."*

What is God's greatest healing of all?

_____

_____

THE SHEPHERD'S CALL

7) **John 13:15** - *"For I gave you an example that you also should do as I did to you."*

From today's scripture, how does **THE** Shepherd inspire **you** to shepherd **your** flock?

_____

_____

MINUTE OF MEDITATION

"Many are the afflictions of the righteous, but the Lord delivers him out of them all" (Psalm 34:19).

PRAYER

Adoration, **C**onfession, **T**hanksgiving, **S**upplication

Perspective

"O clap your hands, all peoples; shout to God with the voice of joy"
(Psalm 47:1).

Psalm 47

The story goes of two elderly men in the last days of their lives who roomed together in a lower room of a hospital for the aged. Both men were confined to bed and limited by the four walls around them. One of the men would wake up each morning and describe the view from the small window directly in front of his bed. His descriptions were vivid and exciting. He talked of birds and butterflies that flew in the sky above. He painted word pictures of children playing outside on a playground. He described sounds of laughter and joyful faces in great detail; the color of their eyes, the description of their hair and colorful clothing. The man was a favorite of the doctors and nurses who cared for him. His days were spent in thanksgiving.

The other man woke up each day irritated and unhappy. He grew more and more jealous because his bed didn't have a picture window. All he could see was a red brick wall on every side. He began to pray that the man with the window would die so he could be moved there. Within a few weeks, his prayer was answered, and his roommate was taken from his picture bed.

As the ungrateful man was transported to the other bed, his face filled with horror as he realized that the other view was just like his. The "window" was only a window of thankful imagination.

1) **Psalm 47:6-7** - *"Sing praises to God, sing praises; sing praises to our King, sing praises. For God is the King of all the earth; sing praises with a skillful psalm."*

   What is it about praise and thanksgiving that brings joy to the heart and adds life to our years?
   _____
   _____

2) **Psalm 47:8-9** - *"God reigns over the nations, God sits on His holy throne. The princes of the people have assembled themselves as the people of the God of Abraham, for the shields of the earth belong to God; He is highly exalted."*

   How can the realization of God's sovereignty remove doubt, fear, and frustration and pave the way for a joyful and peaceful heart?
   _____
   _____

3) **Psalm 100:1-5** - *"Shout joyfully to the Lord, all the earth. Serve the Lord with gladness; come before Him with joyful singing. Know that the Lord Himself is God; it is He who has made us, and not we ourselves; we are His people and the sheep of His pasture. Enter His gates with thanksgiving and His courts with praise. Give thanks to Him, bless His name. For the Lord is good; His lovingkindness is everlasting and His faithfulness to all generations."*

What might daily meditation on this familiar psalm do to your attitude and disposition?

_____

_____

4) **Psalm 138:1-2** - *"I will give You thanks with all my heart; I will sing praises to You before the gods. I will bow down toward Your holy temple and give thanks to Your name for Your lovingkindness and Your truth; for You have magnified Your word according to all Your name."*

How does our thanksgiving bring glory and pleasure to God?

_____

_____

5) **Psalm 138:8** - *"The Lord will accomplish what concerns me; Your lovingkindness, O Lord, is everlasting; do not forsake the works of Your hands."*

What is David communicating to you in this profound passage? What is your emotional response to God's commitment to go before you with the concerns of your heart?

_____

_____

What is your response to His unconditional lovingkindness?

_____

_____

THE SHEPHERD'S CALL

6) **John 13:15** - *"For I gave you an example that you also should do as I did to you."*

From today's scripture, how does **THE** Shepherd inspire **you** to shepherd **your** flock?

_____

_____

"Serve the Lord with gladness; come before Him with joyful singing"
(Psalm 100:2).

PRAYER

Adoration, **C**onfession, **T**hanksgiving, **S**upplication

Grace Restored

"Hide Your face from my sins and blot out all my iniquities" (Psalm 51:9).

Psalm 51

I'll never forget the night at Texas Tech when students who loved Jesus brought a couple of thousand Red Raiders into their basketball arena for our "The Cross" drama. As the students poured out of the bleachers onto the floor at the conclusion, it got crazy. They all began to kneel in rows. There were a lot of tears and brokenness that night on that floor.

As I stepped out amongst the student body to pray with those who needed a shoulder to lean on, I encountered a female student about 5'2" tall with wavy brown hair, beautiful brown eyes, weeping uncontrollably. I asked her what her name was; she said Maggie.

I said, "I already love you, Maggie, that's my granddaughter's name. Why are you crying?"

She said as she looked into my eyes, "When I was 17, I died. The boys took me out, and they raped me and filmed me and made me porn. Since that night, I have fallen again and again and again."

I reached into my back pocket and pulled out the love letter I'd been carrying for the last 20 years. It opened to 2 Corinthians 5:21. I said, "Look, Maggie, it says in here that God made Jesus, who knew no sin, to become rape, become porn, become sin, become all you've gone through, so you could become the righteousness of Christ."

I said, "Maggie, do you know what that means? When you came to the cross tonight, you became Jesus' bride. You became pure--virgin pure. You're pure, Maggie. You're untouched."

Maggie got it. Her face filled with hope. A beautiful, white bridal veil of purity fell on her face from the arena ceiling. No one else saw it, but I did, and Maggie did. When she walked out of that arena, she walked out on a wedding aisle of white rose petals. It was the most beautiful bridal walk you or I will ever see.

That, men and women, is the cross of Jesus. That is why He died there. He died for Maggie.

1) **Psalm 51:1-2** - *"Be gracious to me, O God, according to Your lovingkindness; according to the greatness of Your compassion blot out my transgressions. Wash me thoroughly from my iniquity and cleanse me from my sin."*

Why was Jesus' crucifixion necessary for you personally?

_____

_____

Psalm 51:6 - *"Behold, You desire truth in the innermost being, and in the hidden part You will make me know wisdom."*

What are the "innermost being" and the "hidden part" David is describing here?

_____

_____

Why is the cleansing of the deepest, darkest parts of our souls so *very* necessary for the complete filling of His Spirit?

_____

_____

2) **Psalm 51:7** - *"Purify me with hyssop, and I shall be clean; wash me, and I shall be whiter than snow."*

Describe *grace* as it's portrayed in this passage.

_____

_____

3) **Psalm 51:10-12** - *"Create in me a clean heart, O God, and renew a steadfast spirit within me. Do not cast me away from Your presence and do not take Your Holy Spirit from me. Restore to me the joy of Your salvation and sustain me with a willing spirit."*

This passage could very well be the central outcry and theme of David's heart after his sin with Bathsheba. What is David asking God for in this petition?

_____

_____

For what does your heart cry out in this manner today?

_____

_____

4) **Psalm 138:3** - *"On the day I called, You answered me; You made me bold with strength in my soul."*

What does this passage say about God's *willingness* to hear your cry and His *ability* to restore you?

_____

_____

How is God answering your cry for His miraculous grace in this season of your life?

_____

5) **Psalm 51:13** - *"Then I will teach transgressors Your ways, and sinners will be converted to You."*

What is the connecting word *then* referring to in this verse?

_____

_____

How does the "cleansing and filling" of your spirit enhance your ability to restore the lost sheep you are called to find?

_____

_____

THE SHEPHERD'S CALL

6) **John 13:15** - *"For I gave you an example that you also should do as I did to you."*

From today's scripture, how does **THE** Shepherd inspire **you** to shepherd **your** flock?

_____

_____

MINUTE OF MEDITATION

"Create in me a clean heart, O God, and renew a steadfast spirit within me"
(Psalm 51:10).

PRAYER

Adoration, **C**onfession, **T**hanksgiving, **S**upplication

The Trustworthy Shepherd

"When I am afraid, I will put my trust in You" (Psalm 56:3).

Psalm 56

It's tempting to read the history of the Hebrew nation, from the days of the exodus from Egypt through the times of the judges and kings, and glibly point your finger at their fickle nature toward their Creator and Deliverer. But then we have to look in the mirror and notice how *we* often question God's trustworthiness when tragedy strikes or when He doesn't deliver our desires on a silver platter. We would be in an eternally helpless predicament if God kept track of the times we questioned His trustworthiness and countless efforts to heal, rescue, save, and protect His flock.

I heard the story of a gentleman who was trapped on his rooftop as the rising waters of a flash flood steadily overtook his house and rushed through the neighborhood streets. As the waters crept up the shingles, and he inched his way toward the peak of the roof, he cried out, "God, save me!"

A boat soon passed by his house, rescuing victims from flooded houses. The driver of the boat cried out, "Get in and grab a life jacket!"

The desperate man replied, "God will save me." Then he cried out again, "God, save me!"

Again, another boat drove by with a helping hand. Again, the stranded man replied that God would hear his prayer and rescue him. Surprisingly, it happened yet a third time. Finally, as the man drowned and entered heaven, he stood before God and shook his fist at Him and exclaimed, "Where were You when I cried out to You three times to save me?"

To which God replied, "Where was I? I sent three boats to save you, but you refused to get in."

1) **Psalm 56:4** - *"In God, whose word I praise, in God I have put my trust; I shall not be afraid. What can mere man do to me?"*

   When were you most afraid recently?

   _____
   _____

   How did God respond to your prayer for help?

   _____
   _____

2) **Psalm 56:8-9** - *"You have taken account of my wanderings; put my tears in Your bottle. Are they not in Your book? Then my enemies will turn back in the day when I call; this I know, that God is for me."*

   What is David saying in this beautiful passage about God's tender and purposeful, fatherly care?

   _____
   _____

97

"God is for me." Four simple yet profound words. What do these four words mean to you personally?

_____

_____

3) **Psalm 56:10-11** - *"In God, whose word I praise, in the Lord, whose word I praise, in God I have put my trust, I shall not be afraid. What can man do to me?"*

   Isaiah 26:3-4 - *"The steadfast of mind You will keep in perfect peace, because he trusts in You. Trust in the Lord forever, for in God the Lord, we have an everlasting Rock."*

   Do you trust God some of the time, most of the time, or all the time? Why?

_____

_____

   The amount of fear you experience in this world is directly proportional to the degree of trust you place in the Shepherd who leads you. Why is this age-old, biblically based principle true?

_____

_____

4) **Psalm 37:5** - *"Commit your way to the Lord, trust also in Him, and He will do it."*

   Proverbs 3:5-6 - *"Trust in the Lord with all your heart and do not lean on your own understanding. In all your ways acknowledge Him, and He will make your paths straight."*

   What does it mean to "acknowledge" Him? In addition to that, what do you need to do to deepen your trust in your Shepherd?

_____

_____

   How does trust change your priorities?

_____

_____

5) **Psalm 37:3** - *"Trust in the Lord and do good; dwell in the land and cultivate faithfulness."*

   An old favorite church hymn's lyrics say,
   > "Trust and obey,
   > for there's no other way
   > to be happy in Jesus,
   > but to trust and obey."

   How does trust generate obedience?

_____

_____

How does combining trust and obedience, like part A and part B of epoxy cement, take Jesus' lambs to greener pastures?

_____

_____

THE SHEPHERD'S CALL

6) **John 13:15** - *"For I gave you an example that you also should do as I did to you."*

From today's scripture, how does **THE** Shepherd inspire **you** to shepherd **your** flock?

_____

_____

MINUTE OF MEDITATION
"Commit your way to the Lord, trust also in Him, and He will do it"
(Psalm 37:5).

PRAYER
Adoration, Confession, Thanksgiving, Supplication

<u>Dependence</u>

"For You are my hope; O Lord God, You are my confidence from my youth"
(Psalm 71:5).

Psalm 71

W. Phillip Keller speaks tenderly from the heart of a veteran shepherd as he describes a lamb who has been "cast down" in a helpless position on its back, with its four legs extended skyward and unable to right itself. The animal will soon die due to lack of circulation and the pressure of built-up gas. The patient care the shepherd gives to the helpless lamb, as the lamb is carefully righted onto its feet and its legs are gently caressed to restore circulation, is a pleasant reminder of how God, our Shepherd, reaches out to His sheep when we are brokenhearted and crushed in spirit.

When I was first stricken with leukemia, Satan jumped on the opportunity to break my heart into a million pieces by making me think God was upset with me and wanted to wipe me off the face of the earth. Though I probably deserve it, certainly my Father in heaven has no intention of doing so! The psalmist's comforting words in Psalm 71:3 reassure the wounded heart when we fight emotional battles in times of distress and physical ailments. "He restores my soul" is one of the great promises to those of us who sincerely say, "The Lord is my Shepherd, I shall not want."

1) **Psalm 71:1-2, 14-15 -** *"In You, O Lord, I have taken refuge; let me never be ashamed. In Your righteousness deliver me and rescue me; incline Your ear to me and save me. ... But as for me, I will hope continually, and will praise You yet more and more. My mouth shall tell of Your righteousness and of Your salvation all day long; for I do not know the sum of them."*

Brokenness builds a humble heart. Why is a Christ-follower more filled with praise when his heart is humble and contrite?

_____

_____

Describe a day when you were "cast down" and how "the Good Shepherd" restored your soul.

_____

_____

2) **Psalm 56:13** - *"For You have delivered my soul from death, indeed my feet from stumbling, so that I may walk before God in the light of the living."*

The way God delivers us from our failures, frailties, and falterings should cause us to stand before Him in greater awe, wonder, and praise. Describe a time recently when your realization of your weakness led you to praise Him for His mercy.

_____

_____

3) **Psalm 71:20** - *"You who have shown me many troubles and distresses will revive me again, and will bring me up again from the depths of the earth."*

Describe the true heart of God when one of His sheep falters and cries out to Him in distress. Why does He allow us to experience troubles?

_____

_____

4) **John 15:2b** - *"Every branch that bears fruit, He prunes it so that it may bear more fruit."*

2 Corinthians 4:10 - *"Always carrying about in the body the dying of Jesus, so that the life of Jesus also may be manifested in our body."*

Psalm 71:6 - *"By You I have been sustained from my birth; You are He who took me from my mother's womb; my praise is continually of You."*

Besides allowing us to undergo afflictions, how does God prune us so we'll bear more fruit?

_____

_____

5) **Corinthians 4:16-17** - *"Therefore we do not lose heart, but though our outer man is decaying, yet our inner man is being renewed day by day. For momentary, light affliction is producing for us an eternal weight of glory far beyond all comparison."*

What are some reasons He allows His chosen sheep to experience such great sorrow and affliction?

_____

_____

6) **Psalm 71:23** - *"My lips will shout for joy when I sing praises to You; and my soul, which You have redeemed."*

The Greek word for *redemption* is *exagaridzo,* which means "to be bought out of the slave market, never to go back into slavery again." What does the promise of your redemption in Christ mean to you?

_____

_____

THE SHEPHERD'S CALL

7) **John 13:15** - *"For I gave you an example that you also should do as I did to you."*

From today's scripture, how does **THE** Shepherd inspire **you** to shepherd **your** flock?

_____

_____

MINUTE OF MEDITATION
"In You, O Lord, I have taken refuge; let me never be ashamed. In Your righteousness deliver me and rescue me; incline Your ear to me and save me"
(Psalm 71:1-2).

PRAYER
Adoration, **C**onfession, **T**hanksgiving, **S**upplication

The Nearness of God

"But as for me, the nearness of God is my good; I have made the Lord God my refuge, that I may tell of all Your works" (Psalm 73:28).

Psalm 73

Labrador retrievers are "people dogs." Yes, they can hunt birds, guide the visually impaired, and do excellent narcotics investigation, but they're at their best when they can be close to the master who loves them.

As all my friends know, I have a most-loyal, chocolate lab named Koda. His rich chocolate fur makes him look like a Rocky Mountain Chocolate Factory commercial. We hunt together, fish together, go to work together, ride in the car together, and play together. He is only truly happy if he is no more than one inch away from me. If he's asleep with his head on my foot, he sleeps in peace. That's what "nearness" looks like to me. Oh, how I long for my heart to look like that with my Savior!

The difference between a city dog and a country dog is this: The city dog is penned up all day and all night. He stays by the pen because he has no choice. But if he gets out of his confinement, he runs away, knocks over trash cans, and bites the mailman. (Kidding, of course.) A country dog is free to roam. He enjoys playing in the woods, running in the fields, and splashing in the creek. But you can always find a country dog at night sleeping on the doormat of his master's house, sleeping as close to his master's side as he can get.

It's called "nearness by grace." God sets us free to choose our path and our affection, and He forgives us when we stumble. But in our freedom, we choose to stick as close to His side as we can get. That's our response when we truly appreciate His love unconditional. That's why "the nearness of God" is more valuable, more precious, and more desired than all the riches of the earth and all the other affections this world has to offer.

1) **Psalm 73:23-24** - *"Nevertheless I am continually with You; You have taken hold of my right hand. With Your counsel You will guide me, and afterward receive me to glory."*

   What does "the nearness of God" look like to you?

   _____

   _____

   Is His nearness more precious to you than anything else in your life? Why or why not?

   _____

   _____

   How do you show how much you value His nearness in your daily life?

   _____

   _____

What do you sacrifice to prove that?

_____

_____

2) **Psalm 73:25** - *"Whom have I in heaven but You? And besides You, I desire nothing on earth."*

We may live 70 to 80 or more years on earth, but we will live for eternity in heaven. How does that realization affect your choices and priorities?

_____

_____

3) **Matthew 6:19-21** - *"Do not store up for yourselves treasures on earth, where moth and rust destroy, and where thieves break in and steal. But store up for yourselves treasures in heaven, where neither moth nor rust destroys, and where thieves do not break in or steal; for where your treasure is, there your heart will be also."*

Why does your heart follow the things you treasure the most?

_____

_____

What is your greatest treasure? How do you show it?

_____

_____

4) **Matthew 6:24** - *"No one can serve two masters; for either he will hate the one and love the other, or he will be devoted to one and despise the other. You cannot serve God and wealth."*

Why is it impossible to serve two masters?

_____

_____

Why is life a shallow experience for those who try to put both God and pleasure together as their first love?

_____

_____

5) **Psalm 73:2-3, 16-17** - *"But as for me, my feet came close to stumbling, my steps had almost slipped. For I was envious of the arrogant as I saw the prosperity of the wicked. ... When I pondered to understand this, it was troublesome in my sight until I came into the sanctuary of God; then I perceived their end."*

What is the psalmist confessing in this passage?

_____

_____

Why is the word *until* in verse 17 one of the most weighty words ever written?

_____

_____

THE SHEPHERD'S CALL

6) **John 13:15** - *"For I gave you an example that you also should do as I did to you."*

From today's scripture, how does **THE** Shepherd inspire **you** to shepherd **your** flock?

_____

_____

MINUTE OF MEDITATION

"Nevertheless I am continually with You; You have taken hold of my right hand. With Your counsel You will guide me, and afterward receive me to glory" (Psalm 73:23-24).

PRAYER

Adoration, **C**onfession, **T**hanksgiving, **S**upplication

When God is Silent

"O God, why have You rejected us forever? Why does Your anger smoke against the sheep of Your pasture? Remember Your congregation, which You have purchased of old, which You have redeemed to be the tribe of Your inheritance; and this Mount Zion, where You have dwelt" (Psalm 74:1-2).

Psalm 74

After I graduated from SMU football, I moved to College Station, Texas, and coached the defensive line on the Texas A & M Aggie football team. On the field, it was one of the most-rewarding times of my life. Off the field, it was the greatest horror show I had ever experienced in my 22 years on earth.

Before spring practices began, my college wife of 14 months informed me that she was in love with my best friend. The next morning, she moved back to Dallas. There was no adultery, no porn, no alcohol, none of the surface reasons you might expect. She just felt she had found a better man. I cried almost daily. Some days for hours on end. I felt like my insides were shutting down. I almost lost my will to live. I've never blamed either one of them. I took it all upon myself and saw ways I could have improved as a husband. How I could have treated her with greater honor.

Those days were long and exhausting. Where was God? Why were my prayers for reconciliation not answered? Why was He silent? Truth is, He was never closer by my side. He was carving pride off my life. He was teaching me how to think more of others and less of myself. He was also breaking my heart so I could have a lifetime of ministry to the brokenhearted. My life has been so much deeper and more caring because of the way He allowed me to be broken. I wouldn't trade away those months of sorrow for anything. They were some of the most-necessary days of my life.

1) **Psalm 10:1** - *"Why do You stand afar off, O Lord? Why do You hide Yourself in times of trouble?"*

   Describe a time in your life when you felt God was silent toward you.

   _____

   _____

   How did He later reveal to you that He was with you all along the way?

   _____

   _____

2) **Romans 5:3-5** - *"And not only this, but we also exult in our tribulations, knowing that tribulation brings about perseverance; and perseverance, proven character; and proven character, hope; and hope does not disappoint, because the love of God has been poured out within our hearts through the Holy Spirit who was given to us."*

What did He do to fortify you during those dark days? What lessons did you learn?

_____

_____

3) **Psalm 17:15** - *"As for me, I shall behold Your face in righteousness; I will be satisfied with Your likeness when I awake."*

Psalm 139:11-12 - *"If I say, 'Surely the darkness will overwhelm me, and the light around me will be night,' even the darkness is not dark to You, and the night is as bright as the day. Darkness and light are alike to You."*

Did you seek God's face in your darkest days or turn away? If you sought Him, how did you go about it?

_____

_____

4) **Psalm 74:10-12** - *"How long, O God, will the adversary revile, and the enemy spurn Your name forever? Why do You withdraw Your hand, even Your right hand? From within Your bosom, destroy them! Yet God is my king from of old, who works deeds of deliverance in the midst of the earth."*

In Ohio recently, there was a gathering of various pastors and "Christian" leaders at a Planned Parenthood abortion clinic to give a "faith blessing" for the workers and clients. The headline on the press notice from Planned Parenting read, "Holy Ground: Blessing the Sacred Space of Decision." When the adversary seems to run freely throughout our nation and the enemies of God speak out boldly, how and why do we proclaim God's greatness?

_____

_____

5) **Psalm 76:7-9** - *"You, even You, are to be feared; and who may stand in Your presence when once You are angry? You caused judgment to be heard from heaven; the earth feared and was still when God arose to judgment, to save all the humble of the earth."*

Philippians 2:9-11 - *"For this reason also, God highly exalted Him, and bestowed on Him the name which is above every name, so that at the name of Jesus every knee will bow, of those who are in heaven and on earth and under the earth, and that every tongue will confess that Jesus Christ is Lord, to the glory of God the Father."*

Describe the supremacy of God and His final rule over all mankind. What comfort does His sovereignty and ultimate dominion bring you in your times of distress?

_____

_____

6) **Psalm 103:3-5** - *"Who pardons all your iniquities, who heals all your diseases; who redeems your life from the pit, who crowns you with lovingkindness and compassion; who satisfies your years with good things, so that your youth is renewed like the eagle."*

How does His graceful, purposeful, healing hand bring hope to your heart when life's challenges come crashing down?

_____

_____

THE SHEPHERD'S CALL

7) **John 13:15** - *"For I gave you an example that you also should do as I did to you."*

From today's scripture, how does **THE** Shepherd inspire **you** to shepherd **your** flock?

_____

_____

MINUTE OF MEDITATION
"And not only this, but we also exult in our tribulations, knowing that tribulation brings about perseverance; and perseverance, proven character; and proven character, hope; and hope does not disappoint, because the love of God has been poured out within our hearts through the Holy Spirit who was given to us" (Romans 5:3-5).

PRAYER
Adoration, **C**onfession, **T**hanksgiving, **S**upplication

The Face of God

"Oh, give ear, Shepherd of Israel, You who lead Joseph like a flock; You who are enthroned above the cherubim, shine forth" (Psalm 80:1).

Psalm 80

Face to Face with Jesus

There's a little child inside of you;
with dreams naïve, his hope is new.

His belief unmarred, his heart unstained;
says "Abba, Daddy," his love proclaimed.

He reaches upward, his eyes are sure;
his dad's embrace, his faith is pure.

His father's love now face to face;
enthralling trust, his dad's embrace.

His emotions trusting, they know no pain;
sweet affirmation his highest aim.

The sun sets nightly, the moon's arising;
the days, now years, bring trials realizing.

Through disappointments and people's sin;
his conscience marred and hurt within.

Staunch confrontation, the world's embrace;
the child part of a fallen race.

Yet looking back he soon realizes;
his deepest hope, his faith arises.

He finds in Jesus and the crucifixion;
the grace of God and His benediction.

His heart transformed, the Spirit's power;
his longing grows with every hour.

Oh childlike faith, his invitation;
now Abba Jesus, fresh realization.

Tho' sin exists, God's grace abounding;
consuming love, His heart confounding.

God's intimate love, so deeply yearning;
his childlike faith, hence now returning.

Now face to face, his spirit willing;
the Spirit's power, his heart fulfilling.

Hence, face to face with Jesus, His night in the Upper Room;
going back in time, His love sublime, our debt He would assume.

Face to face with Jesus, as He washes your soiled feet;
down on His knees, the Father pleased, your cleansing to complete.

Face to face with Jesus, the garden of Gethsemane;
the Father's Son, "thy will be done," they nailed Him to the tree.

Oh face to face with Jesus, the trials throughout the night;
God's plan in place, your love slaps to His face, in worship we recite.

Face to face with Jesus, the scourging of the whip;
oh glory be, our purity, our forgiveness to equip.

Face to face with Jesus, in pain He carries the cross;
longsuffering quakes, each step He takes, our gain becomes His loss.

Oh face to face with Jesus, the crowning of His head;
for you and me, humility, His blood in flowing red.

Face to face with Jesus, the nails of crucifixion;
His wrists and feet, our ransom complete, display of sin's conviction.

Now face to face with Jesus, it's ours in His resurrection; in moments of
gold, His face behold, He is our daily reflection.

Oh look into His eyes, and see the Father's love;
we're not condemned, He is our friend, God's gift from up above.

Oh look into His Word, in deepest meditation;
you'll see His face, a fond embrace, His highest invitation.

He looks into your heart today, the window to your soul;
no longer blamed, we're not ashamed, His embrace our greatest goal.

1) **Psalm 80:3** - *"O God, restore us and cause Your face to shine upon us,
and we will be saved."*

How big is God? If NASA estimates that the known cosmos is a
startling 27.4 billion light years in diameter, then God is, at the very
least, bigger than that! Yet when we go face to face with Him, we see
His face shine in warmth, lovingkindness, and affection. What is
David asking for in this passage?

_____

_____

115

2) **Numbers 6:25-26** - *"The Lord make His face shine on you, and be gracious to you; the Lord lift up His countenance on you, and give you peace."*

What does it mean that the Lord would "make His face shine on you"?

_____

_____

Why would you want God to make His face shine on you?

_____

_____

3) **Exodus 33:11** - *"Thus the Lord used to speak to Moses face to face, just as a man speaks to his friend. When Moses returned to the camp, his servant Joshua, the son of Nun, a young man, would not depart from the tent."*

How does this verse speak to your heart about *your* potential to experience God's "face to face" friendship?

_____

_____

How could it change your communication with God?

_____

_____

4) **2 Corinthians 4:6** - *"For God, who said, 'Light shall shine out of darkness,' is the One who has shone in our hearts to give the Light of the knowledge of the glory of God in the face of Christ."*

If God spoke to Moses as a friend and shined on David, Noah, Peter, Paul, the thief on the cross, and countless other broken, undeserving individuals, what does it mean to you that He put that "shine" of glory in your heart?

_____

_____

What do you need to do with that realization?

_____

_____

THE SHEPHERD'S CALL

5) **John 13:15** - *"For I gave you an example that you also should do as I did to you."*

From today's scripture, how does **THE** Shepherd inspire **you** to shepherd **your** flock?

_____

_____

MINUTE OF MEDITATION
"Thus the Lord used to speak to Moses face to face, just as a man speaks to his friend" (Exodus 33:11a).

PRAYER
Adoration, **C**onfession, **T**hanksgiving, **S**upplication

Listen!

*"Hear, O My people, and I will admonish you; O Israel,
if you would listen to Me"* (Psalm 81:8).

Psalm 81

Two ears, one mouth. The ratio says everything!
You want a good relationship with your parents? Listen!
You want a great marriage? Listen!
You want to be a great parent? Listen!
You want to do well professionally? Listen!
You want to solve conflict? Listen!
You want to go deep in a relationship? Listen!
You want to live in peace? Listen!
You want a high G.P.A.? Listen!
You want to be an effective leader? Listen!
And ... you want a *great* relationship with God?
L-I-S-T-E-N!

In terms of relationships, "listen" may well be the most-significant six-letter word ever written--and perhaps the term most-easily overlooked.

Our listening capacity is almost limitless. The human ear has more circuit potential than all of New York City combined!

In John 10:27, Jesus says, *"My sheep hear My voice, and I know them, and they follow Me."* The lamb that listens to the shepherd's voice and obeys his commands finds green pasture and grows to provide many cuttings of wool for his master. The lamb that ignores the shepherd's call gets lost from the flock and perishes in the fangs of the predator.

1) **Psalm 81:11-12** - *"But My people did not listen to My voice, and Israel did not obey Me. So I gave them over to the stubbornness of their heart, to walk in their own devices."*

   What does it mean to be "given over" by God? Could anything be more horrible to experience than for God to "give us over" to the stubbornness of our hearts?

   _____

   What does it mean to listen to God's voice? How does good listening to Him keep us from that awful fate?

   _____

2) **Isaiah 55:2b-3a** - *"Listen carefully to Me. ... Incline your ear and come to Me. Listen, that you may live; and I will make an everlasting covenant with you."*

   What's the benefit of using good listening skills in your relationship with God?

   _____

   _____

3) **2 Timothy 3:16** - *"All Scripture is inspired by God and profitable for teaching, for reproof, for correction, for training in righteousness."*

   John 16:13 - *"But when He, the Spirit of truth, comes, He will guide you into all the truth; for He will not speak on His own initiative, but whatever He hears, He will speak; and He will disclose to you what is to come."*

   How do Scripture and the Spirit help us to hear God's voice?
   _____
   _____

   How well are you listening to God's Word and the Holy Spirit?
   _____
   _____

4) **Psalm 81:13-14** - *"Oh that My people would listen to Me, that Israel would walk in My ways! I would quickly subdue their enemies and turn My hand against their adversaries."*

   What are God's rewards for good listening skills as they apply to our relationship with Him?
   _____
   _____

5) **James 1:19** - *"This you know, my beloved brethren. But everyone must be quick to hear, slow to speak and slow to anger."*

   What is God saying to you in terms of your practice (or lack) of good listening skills?
   _____
   _____

   How can you improve?
   _____
   _____

THE SHEPHERD'S CALL

6) **John 13:15** - *"For I gave you an example that you also should do as I did to you."*

   From today's scripture, how does **THE** Shepherd inspire **you** to shepherd **your** flock?
   _____
   _____

MINUTE OF MEDITATION

"Listen carefully to Me. ... Incline your ear and come to Me.
Listen, that you may live" (Isaiah 55:2b-3a).

PRAYER

Adoration, **C**onfession, **T**hanksgiving, **S**upplication

The Greenest Pasture of All

"How lovely are Your dwelling places, O Lord of hosts! My soul longed and even yearned for the courts of the Lord; my heart and my flesh sing for joy to the living God" (Psalm 84:1-2).

Psalm 84

Whoever coined the phrase "The grass is always greener on the other side of the fence" was right up there with the one who first asked, "Why did the chicken cross the road?" There have been almost as many spinoffs of the first phrase as there have been jokes about the second. "When the grass is greener on the other side of the fence, there must be a sewer leak somewhere" has to be my favorite. I've spent my entire adult life watching men and women bounce from religion to religion, relationship to relationship, job to job, position to position, spouse to spouse, hobby to hobby, and countless other fickle naiveties, trying to find happiness, when a lot of prayer and hard work would green up the grass in the pasture where God had already placed them.

After 70 years of watching countless frustrated people sticking their necks through barbed wire fences, looking for the elusive treasure on the other side, one thing is absolutely true without any exception: In God's Word lies the greenest grass of all. There is no pasture for a hungry lamb that is more nourishing, more fulfilling, more rewarding, more inspiring, and more satisfying than the grass that grows just beside the feet of the Shepherd. The psalmists saw that green grass as "the courts of the Lord."

1) **Psalm 84:4** - *"How blessed are those who dwell in Your house! They are ever praising You."*

   In the psalmists' day, the Hebrew nation found God in the Tabernacle, where God came to earth in the Holy of Holies, the place of the sacred law. Where do believers find God today?

   _____

   _____

2) **Psalm 84:5** - *"How blessed is the man whose strength is in You, in whose heart are the highways to Zion!"*

   In the psalmists' vocabulary, Zion was the place of the Tabernacle, in the heart of Jerusalem. What does a person's heart look like when it's filled with roads that *all* lead to the heart of God?

   _____

   _____

Psalm 84:10a - *"For a day in Your courts is better than a thousand outside."*

You can *feel* the psalmists desperately pressing into the nearness of God, like a lamb pressing into the closeness of his shepherd. What does this oft-quoted phrase tell you about "the greenest grass" of *your* heart's desire?

_____

_____

3) **Psalm 84:10b** - *"I would rather stand at the threshold of the house of my God than dwell in the tents of wickedness."*

What are the psalmists saying in this passage? How do you apply it to your life today?

_____

_____

4) **Psalm 23:2a** - *"He makes me lie down in green pastures."*

Why does the Great Shepherd have to "make" you lie down in green pastures?

_____

_____

Why do we tend to wander away from the pasture He chooses for us to rest in?

_____

_____

5) **Psalm 84:11-12** - *"For the Lord God is a sun and shield; the Lord gives grace and glory; no good thing does He withhold from those who walk uprightly. O Lord of hosts, how blessed is the man who trusts in You!"*

How can complete trust in "the heart of the Shepherd" eliminate worry and fear?

_____

_____

THE SHEPHERD'S CALL

6) **John 13:15** - *"For I gave you an example that you also should do as I did to you."*

From today's scripture, how does **THE** Shepherd inspire **you** to shepherd **your** flock?

_____

_____

MINUTE OF MEDITATION
"For a day in Your courts is better than a thousand outside. I would rather stand at the threshold of the house of my God than dwell in the tents of wickedness" (Psalm 84:10).

PRAYER
Adoration, Confession, Thanksgiving, Supplication

Restoring the Lambs

"You forgave the iniquity of Your people; You covered all their sin"
(Psalm 85:2).

Psalm 85

In the days of Roman rule in the Western world, the prisons were horrible, and the conditions for prisoners were deplorable. When a violator of Roman law was evaluated by the governor, punishment was often swift and severe. In the judgments that required imprisonment, the accused would be issued a "certificate of debt," which would sometimes hang outside the cell door on a clay tablet inscribed with the terms of punishment. At the completion of the sentence, the term *Tetelestai* would be inscribed across the certificate of debt, which meant the debt had been "paid in full." The prisoner would carry the tablet with him as he left the jail so that if anyone tried to accuse him again of the crime, he could show the tablet and prove his debt had been paid. He could never be tried for that infraction again.

Colossians 2:13-14 speaks of the sin debt we owed and how Jesus paid the price for it on the cross: *"When you were dead in your transgressions and the uncircumcision of your flesh, He made you alive together with Him, having forgiven us all our transgressions, having canceled out the certificate of debt consisting of decrees against us, which was hostile to us; and He has taken it out of the way, having nailed it to the cross."*

John 19:30 records the historical statement that is forever proclaimed on our eternal behalf: *"Therefore when Jesus had received the sour wine, He said, 'It is finished [Tetelestai]!' And He bowed His head and gave up His spirit."*

Tetelestai--our debt is paid in full. "It [Jesus' mission of forgiveness] is finished."

1) Write a sentence in ten words or less, from your heart to the heart of the Great Shepherd, letting Him know what His *Tetelestai* proclamation means to you.

   _____

   _____

2) **Psalm 85:4** - *"Restore us, O God of our salvation, and cause Your indignation toward us to cease."*

   How does God's grace restore you, motivate you, enrich your spirit, and fill your soul?

   _____

   _____

3) **Psalm 85:5** - *"Will You be angry with us forever? Will You prolong Your anger to all generations?"*

How did Jesus' decision to become the Lamb of God answer this question?

_____

_____

4) **Psalm 85:7-8** - *"Show us Your lovingkindness, O Lord, and grant us Your salvation. I will hear what God the Lord will say; for He will speak peace to His people, to His godly ones; but let them not turn back to folly."*

If we truly understand God's forgiveness, it should bring peace to our souls. Do you experience that peace? Why or why not?

_____

_____

Why should grace motivate us to live in freedom from sin?

_____

_____

5) **Psalm 85:9-10, 13** - *"Surely His salvation is near to those who fear Him, that glory may dwell in our land. Lovingkindness and truth have met together; righteousness and peace have kissed each other. ... Righteousness will go before Him and will make His footsteps into a way."*

Think about the golden chain of keywords in this passage: *salvation, fear* God, God's *glory, lovingkindness, truth, righteousness, peace.* If you "bind this golden chain around your neck daily," what will happen to your core values, your moral standards, and your reverence for God's grace?

_____

_____

THE SHEPHERD'S CALL

6) **John 13:15** - *"For I gave you an example that you also should do as I did to you."*

From today's scripture, how does **THE** Shepherd inspire **you** to shepherd **your** flock?

_____

_____

127

MINUTE OF MEDITATION
"You forgave the iniquity of Your people; You covered all their sin"
(Psalm 85:2).

PRAYER
Adoration, **C**onfession, **T**hanksgiving, **S**upplication

Lovingkindness

"I will sing of the lovingkindness of the Lord forever; to all generations I will make known Your faithfulness with my mouth" (Psalm 89:1).

"For where a covenant is, there must of necessity be the death of the one who made it" (Hebrews 9:16).

Psalm 89

No one understood the terms of the biblical covenant better than David. In 1 Samuel 18:3, he made his historic covenant with Jonathan: *"Then Jonathan made a covenant with David because he loved him as himself."* In 2 Samuel 7:16, David was gracefully granted a covenant with God: *"Your house and your kingdom shall endure before Me forever; your throne shall be established forever."*

One of the terms used in the declaration of a biblical covenant is *lovingkindness*, which means, "I love you based solely on *what I do for you.*" Lovingkindness is not love based on "what you do for me," which is seen in broken friendships and broken homes today. In the postmodern Christian culture, it's more often defined as "I love you *if* you'll do this for me" or "I love you *because* you do this for me." But true lovingkindness says, "I love you based on the fact that I *choose* to love you" or "I love you *regardless*" or "I love you, *period.*" Taking it one step further, lovingkindness says, "The more I do for you, the more I love you."

1) **Psalm 89:2-4** - *"For I have said, 'Lovingkindness will be built up forever; in the heavens You will establish Your faithfulness.' 'I have made a covenant with My chosen; I have sworn to David My servant, I will establish your seed forever and build up your throne to all generations.'"*

   What were the terms of the covenant God made with David?
   _____
   _____

   What did David do to deserve such a promise?
   _____
   _____

   Why do you think God chose to express His lovingkindness to David, even after David's sin with Bathsheba?
   _____
   _____

2) **Romans 5:8** - *"But God demonstrates His own love toward us, in that while we were yet sinners, Christ died for us."*

   Titus 3:4-6 - *"But when the kindness of God our Savior and His love for mankind appeared, He saved us, not on the basis of deeds which we have done in righteousness, but according to His mercy, by the washing of regeneration and renewing by the Holy Spirit, whom He poured out upon us richly through Jesus Christ our Savior."*

   How do these passages define God's lovingkindness toward us in the death of His Son?

   _____

   _____

3) **Psalm 89:20-22** - *"I have found David My servant; with My holy oil I have anointed him, with whom My hand will be established; My arm also will strengthen him. The enemy will not deceive him, nor the son of wickedness afflict him."*

   How have you, having found the lovingkindness of God through your faith in Jesus, witnessed evidence of God's unconditional love?

   _____

   _____

4) **Psalm 89:30-33** - *"If his sons forsake My law and do not walk in My judgments, if they violate My statutes and do not keep My commandments, then I will punish their transgression with the rod and their iniquity with stripes. But I will not break off My lovingkindness from him, nor deal falsely in My faithfulness."*

   As the Roman guards beat the crown of thorns into Jesus' brow with rods and laid out stripes of blood across His back with the scourge, He was paying the price for our sin prescribed in Psalm 89. What feelings does that truth stir in you?

   _____

   _____

5) **Psalm 86:8-10** - *"There is no one like You among the gods, O Lord, nor are there any works like Yours. All nations whom You have made shall come and worship before You, O Lord, and they shall glorify Your name. For You are great and do wondrous deeds; You alone are God."*

   What is our proper response to the lovingkindness of God?

   _____

   _____

THE SHEPHERD'S CALL

6) **John 13:15** - *"For I gave you an example that you also should do as I did to you."*

From today's scripture, how does **THE** Shepherd inspire **you** to shepherd **your** flock?

_____

_____

MINUTE OF MEDITATION

"But when the kindness of God our Savior and His love for mankind appeared, He saved us, not on the basis of deeds which we have done in righteousness, but according to His mercy, by the washing of regeneration and renewing by the Holy Spirit, whom He poured out upon us richly through Jesus Christ our Savior" (Titus 3:4-6).

PRAYER
Adoration, **C**onfession, **T**hanksgiving, **S**upplication

Carpe Diem

"So teach us to number our days, that we may present to You a heart of wisdom" (Psalm 90:12).

Psalm 90

Originating with the Roman poet Horace, written in 23 BC, the Latin aphorism *Carpe Diem* has been translated "Seize the day" and used through the centuries in books and letters to motivate one another to never waste a minute, for time is as fleeting as the wind.

You see, every morning you're given a check of highest value for 86,400 seconds that can be spent, invested, or wasted at your discretion. At the end of the day, the check is valued at zero, with nothing held over to be spent the next day. You're only guaranteed one check for your entire lifetime. God never promised tomorrow, only today.

There are a million ways to waste time, your most-valuable commodity, but only one way to invest it to yield the highest return: to pour God's Word and God's love into the life of someone else so he or she can pour it into another. It's called "legacy." It's the best investment of a lifetime.

1) **Psalm 90:1-4** - *"Lord, You have been our dwelling place in all generations. Before the mountains were born or You gave birth to the earth and the world, even from everlasting to everlasting, You are God. You turn man back into dust and say, 'Return, O children of men.' For a thousand years in Your sight are like yesterday when it passes by, or as a watch in the night."*

   What does this passage say about the attributes of God?

   _____

   _____

2) **Psalm 90:5-6** - *"You have swept them away like a flood, they fall asleep; in the morning they are like grass which sprouts anew. In the morning it flourishes and sprouts anew; toward evening it fades and withers away."*

   Psalm 103:15-16 - *"As for man, his days are like grass; as a flower of the field, so he flourishes. When the wind has passed over it, it is no more, and its place acknowledges it no longer."*

   What are Moses (Psalm 90) and David (Psalm 103) affirming about length of life?

   _____

   _____

3) **Psalm 90:9-10** - *"For all our days have declined in Your fury; we have finished our years like a sigh. As for the days of our life, they contain seventy years, or if due to strength, eighty years, yet their pride is but labor and sorrow; for soon it is gone and we fly away."*

Why is investing in things of eternal value the only rational use of our 86,400-second daily check?

_____

_____

How are you doing with your daily priorities?

_____

_____

4) **Psalm 90:12** - *"So teach us to number our days, that we may present to You a heart of wisdom."*

How does your use of your precious minutes need to change?

_____

_____

5) **Psalm 90:16-17** - *"Let Your work appear to Your servants and Your majesty to their children. Let the favor of the Lord our God be upon us; and confirm for us the work of our hands; yes, confirm the work of our hands."*

How do you plan to best invest your time for the rest of your life to yield the highest dividends possible?

_____

_____

THE SHEPHERD'S CALL
6) **John 13:15** - *"For I gave you an example that you also should do as I did to you."*

From today's scripture, how does **THE** Shepherd inspire **you** to shepherd **your** flock?

_____

_____

MINUTE OF MEDITATION
"So teach us to number our days, that we may present to You a heart of wisdom" (Psalm 90:12).

PRAYER
Adoration, **C**onfession, **T**hanksgiving, **S**upplication

God: the Shepherd-in-Chief

"He who dwells in the shelter of the Most High will abide in the shadow of the Almighty. I will say to the Lord, 'My refuge and my fortress, My God, in whom I trust'" (Psalm 91:1-2).

Psalm 91

Two short Bible verses: four names for God--powerful, pivotal, personal scripture at its highest level.
- Most High God
- Almighty God
- Lord God
- My God

Most High God - In Hebrew, *El Elyon* means "the supremacy of God over all other gods."
"That they may know that You alone, whose name is the Lord, are the Most High over all the earth" (Psalm 83:18).

Almighty God - This is translated from the Hebrew name *El Shaddai*, or "God, the all-powerful One."
The term *omnipotent* describes "Almighty God" well. He has all the power He needs to do anything He desires to do. As spoken to Abraham, God said, *"I am God Almighty; walk before Me, and be blameless"* (Genesis 17:1).

Lord - This term is usually used when God's proper name is meant. The Hebrew without vowels is *YHWH*. Other translations are "Yahweh" or "Jehovah." As God spoke to Abraham, *"Is anything too difficult for the Lord? At the appointed time I will return to you, at this time next year, and Sarah will have a son"* (Genesis 18:14).

My God - The Hebrew word *Elohim* simply means "God." *"In the beginning God created the heavens and the earth"* (Genesis 1:1). "My God" makes our Creator personal and knowable. Jesus spoke in the most-well-known prayer in all the world, *"Our* Father who art in heaven." All-knowing, all-present, all-powerful He is! But "All-Knowable" may very well be the most endearing name of all!

1) **Psalm 91:2-4** - *"I will say to the Lord, 'My refuge and my fortress, My God, in whom I trust!' For it is He who delivers you from the snare of the trapper and from the deadly pestilence. He will cover you with His pinions, and under His wings you may seek refuge. His faithfulness is a shield and bulwark."*

   Here the psalmist pictures the protective Shepherd as a giant eagle. Describe the sense of security you feel walking in fellowship with God.

   _____

   _____

Why is that important to you?

_____

_____

2) **Psalm 91:5-6** - *"You will not be afraid of the terror by night, or of the arrow that flies by day; of the pestilence that stalks in darkness, or of the destruction that lays waste at noon."*

Gary Smalley once said that fear is "temporary atheism." Why is that true?

_____

_____

3) **Psalm 91:9-12** - *"For you have made the Lord, my refuge, even the Most High, your dwelling place. No evil will befall you, nor will any plague come near your tent. For He will give His angels charge concerning you, to guard you in all your ways. They will bear you up in their hands, that you do not strike your foot against a stone."*

Why can you trust God even in the midst of tragedy?

_____

_____

4) **Psalm 91:14-15** - *"Because he has loved Me, therefore I will deliver him; I will set him securely on high, because he has known My name. He will call upon Me, and I will answer him; I will be with him in trouble; I will rescue him and honor him."*

What's the difference between trusting God in your head and trusting Him in your heart?

_____

_____

If you truly trust Him in your heart, what "thought choices" will you make when ...

Somebody hurts you?	Anger or Grace
Something negative occurs?	Stress or Peace
Somebody confronts you?	Anger or Openness
Someone disappoints you?	Mercy or Bitterness
Life seems unfair?	Whine or Trust

5) **Psalm 91:16** - *"With a long life I will satisfy him and let him see My salvation."*

What did this psalm say to you that you needed to hear today?

_____

_____

THE SHEPHERD'S CALL

6) **John 13:15** - *"For I gave you an example that you also should do as I did to you."*

From today's scripture, how does **THE** Shepherd inspire **you** to shepherd **your** flock?

_____

_____

MINUTE OF MEDITATION

"Because he has loved Me, therefore I will deliver him; I will set him securely on high, because he has known My name. He will call upon Me, and I will answer him; I will be with him in trouble; I will rescue him and honor him"
(Psalm 91:14-15).

PRAYER

Adoration, **C**onfession, **T**hanksgiving, **S**upplication

Fertile Soil

"The righteous man will flourish like the palm tree, he will grow like a cedar in Lebanon" (Psalm 92:12).

Psalm 92

I memorized this short poem 62 years ago; I never forgot it:

> "A toadstool grows up overnight,
> Learn the lesson little folk.
> An oak it grows 100 years,
> But then it is an oak."

Growing up in "clay country," digging post holes with handheld post hole diggers in southeast Texas, was almost impossible, with concrete-hard red clay lying in layers just beneath the surface. That red clay has laid many a blister on the hands of cattle farmers who embarked on fence-building in the Brazos County of my youth.

Moving to southwest Missouri and continuing my quest to dig post holes and plant trees was no vacation either! In Taney County and Stone County, Missouri, the issue is rock ... brick-hard limestone either on the surface or often just below. They don't call it *Stone* County for nothing. It has earned its reputation! If it's not solid rock, it's prolific chunks of rock and subsurface boulders that make digging a nightmare for the farmers and tree-planters alike.

Earnie Bohner is the hardest-working man I know. This dear, godly man has fulfilled his dream to bring and maintain a picturesque and highly productive blueberry and blackberry farm in the heart of Stone County, Missouri. That man has worked his hands and fingers into rough, solid calluses from four decades of introducing imported topsoil, fertilizers, and mulch by the truckload above the stony, stubborn subsoil. I take my hat off to that dear man. Turning rocky soil into fertile farming soil is surely one of the most-difficult jobs in America. Hats off to you, Earnie! You've taught me a lot about work, life, and godly living.

1) **Jeremiah 17:8** - *"For he will be like a tree planted by the water, that extends its roots by a stream and will not fear when the heat comes; but its leaves will be green, and it will not be anxious in a year of drought nor cease to yield fruit."*

   Psalm 1:3 - *"He will be like a tree firmly planted by streams of water, which yields its fruit in its season and its leaf does not wither; and in whatever he does, he prospers."*

   What are the common elements in these descriptions by Jeremiah and the psalmist?

   _____

   _____

What is required for a tree to stand firmly in a hurricane or the heat of summer?

_____

_____

What do you need to do to make the rest of your life a giant, fruit-bearing, storm-resistant tree?

_____

_____

2) **Psalm 92:6-7** - *"A senseless man has no knowledge, nor does a stupid man understand this: that when the wicked sprouted up like grass and all who did iniquity flourished, it was only that they might be destroyed forevermore."*

Why does wickedness sprout up quickly while goodness takes a lifetime to grow?

_____

_____

3) **Matthew 13:3-9** - *"And He spoke many things to them in parables, saying, 'Behold, the sower went out to sow; and as he sowed, some seeds fell beside the road, and the birds came and ate them up. Others fell on the rocky places, where they did not have much soil; and immediately they sprang up, because they had no depth of soil. But when the sun had risen, they were scorched; and because they had no root, they withered away. Others fell among the thorns, and the thorns came up and choked them out. And others fell on the good soil and yielded a crop, some a hundredfold, some sixty, and some thirty. He who has ears, let him hear."*

What makes a person's heart "fertile soil"? Why is fertile soil essential to growth in regard to a believer's becoming "a tree firmly planted"?

_____

_____

What are the ingredients of fertile soil? Stretch yourself; fill in all ten:

1. **Proverbs 9:9** - *"Give instruction to a wise man and he will be still wiser, teach a righteous man and he will increase his learning."*

   _____

2. **2 Timothy 2:2** - *"The things which you have heard from me in the presence of many witnesses, entrust these to faithful men who will be able to teach others also."*

   _____

3. **2 Timothy 3:16-17** - *"All Scripture is inspired by God and profitable for teaching, for reproof, for correction, for training in righteousness; so that the man of God may be adequate, equipped for every good work."*

4. **1 Thessalonians 5:18** - *"In everything give thanks; for this is God's will for you in Christ Jesus."*

5. **Jeremiah 29:12** - *"Then you will call upon Me and come and pray to Me, and I will listen to you."*

6. **2 Chronicles 16:9a** - *"For the eyes of the Lord move to and fro throughout the earth that He may strongly support those whose heart is completely His."*

7. **2 Timothy 1:7** - *"For God has not given us a spirit of timidity, but of power and love and discipline."*

8. **Matthew 28:19** - *"Go therefore and make disciples of all the nations, baptizing them in the name of the Father and the Son and the Holy Spirit."*

9. **Hebrews 10:24-25** - *"And let us consider how to stimulate one another to love and good deeds, not forsaking our own assembling together, as is the habit of some, but encouraging one another; and all the more as you see the day drawing near."*

10. **Acts 1:8** - *"But you will receive power when the Holy Spirit has come upon you; and you shall be My witnesses both in Jerusalem, and in all Judea and Samaria, and even to the remotest part of the earth."*

THE SHEPHERD'S CALL

4) **John 13:15** - *"For I gave you an example that you also should do as I did to you."*

From today's scripture, how does **THE** Shepherd inspire **you** to shepherd **your** flock?

MINUTE OF MEDITATION

"He will be like a tree firmly planted by streams of water, which yields its fruit in its season and its leaf does not wither; and in whatever he does, he prospers" (Psalm 1:3).

PRAYER

Adoration, Confession, Thanksgiving, Supplication

Majesty

"The Lord reigns, He is clothed with majesty; the Lord has clothed and girded Himself with strength; indeed, the world is firmly established, it will not be moved" (Psalm 93:1).

Psalm 93

No surprise, but the word *majesty* comes from the Greek word *mega*, which means "BIG."

Size – Awe-inspiring
Power - Beyond human comprehension
Knowledge - Limitless
Call it OMNI-EVERYTHING!

God has the artistic quality to paint a rainbow, design a star, and form a snowflake crystal different from all others ever designed, with more unmatched, microscopic intricacy than any human artist could ever dream of.

He has the brilliance to be able to pack 3 billion biological components into a DNA molecule. Though only one 13-billion trillionth the size of an Apple watch, this God-designed DNA machine can do things the Apple will never begin to accomplish.

He has the power to spin our earth on its axis at a speed of 1,000 miles per hour, race it around the sun at 67,000 miles per hour, and drive our entire solar system through our galaxy at the blinding speed of 515,000 miles per hour while rocking a baby sparrow to sleep in her fragile nest of twigs and straw until her wings are ready to fly. Majestic wonder!

Perhaps most remarkable of all, He still has enough wisdom left over to weave even our greatest failures into a home-spun tapestry that looks more and more like His likeness every day of our lives.

1) **Psalm 93:2** - *"Your throne is established from of old; You are from everlasting."*

   A god small enough for us to fully understand could never be big enough to worship. How does God's mysterious, everlasting nature draw you to Him in worship?

   _____

   _____

2) **Psalm 93:4b-5** - *"The Lord on high is mighty. Your testimonies are fully confirmed; holiness befits Your house, O Lord, forevermore."*

   God's strength, God's laws, God's holiness. Describe how these three attributes of God hold up His deity like three perfect legs of a "theistic tripod."

   _____

   _____

3) **1 Chronicles 29:11** - *"Yours, O Lord, is the greatness and the power and the glory and the victory and the majesty, indeed everything that is in the heavens and the earth; Yours is the dominion, O Lord, and You exalt Yourself as head over all."*

What is God communicating to you in this passage? Describe how it influences your feelings for Him.

_____

_____

4) **Hebrews 1:3-4** - *"And He is the radiance of His glory and the exact representation of His nature, and upholds all things by the word of His power. When He had made purification of sins, He sat down at the right hand of the Majesty on high, having become as much better than the angels, as He has inherited a more excellent name than they."*

How does Jesus embody God's majesty?

_____

_____

5) **Micah 5:4** - *"And He will arise and shepherd His flock in the strength of the Lord, in the majesty of the name of the Lord His God. And they will remain, because at that time He will be great to the ends of the earth."*

In referring to this passage, expositor John Gill writes, "The reference here spoken of can be of no other than The Messiah. ... He is both King and Shepherd. ... Christ feeds His flock, He leads them out in God's pastures, protects them from all their enemies, He feeds them with Himself, The Bread of Life ... and all this, 'in the strength of The Lord.' And with His gospel, the rod of His strength, and in such manner as to defend His flock from all that would devour them: *In the majesty of the name of the Lord His God*" (emphasis added).

How does this prophetic description of Jesus the Messiah bring the majesty of God "down to earth" and personalize it for you?

_____

_____

THE SHEPHERD'S CALL

6) **John 13:15** - *"For I gave you an example that you also should do as I did to you."*

From today's scripture, how does **THE** Shepherd inspire **you** to shep herd **your** flock?

_____

_____

MINUTE OF MEDITATION
"He will be like a tree firmly planted by streams of water, which yields its fruit in its season and its leaf does not wither; and in whatever he does, he prospers" (Psalm 1:3).

PRAYER
Adoration, Confession, Thanksgiving, Supplication

Interlude

"Woe, shepherds of Israel who have been feeding themselves! Should not the shepherds feed the flock?" (Ezekiel 34:2b)

Ezekiel 34

Dallas Willard calls *it* "The Great Omission." The Bible calls *it* "The Great Commission." Jesus called *it* "Plan A for reaching the lost world." *It* was the first job He did when He began His public ministry. He spent well over 90% of His vital three-year ministry span focusing on *it*.

What is *it*? Making disciples. Building long-term relationships and intentionally pouring God's Word into another's heart. Mentoring and shepherding your flock. Feeding the sheep. In Jesus' infamous upper-room discourse, His final words to His disciples on the night He was arrested, He declared five times, *"If you love me, you will keep my commandments."* *"Go make disciples"* was his last command. These "famous last words" have motivated millions of saints over the years to give their lives to make Jesus known to the world.

If you spoke to 10,000 people every night, 365 nights every year, about Jesus and every person gave their heart to Him, it would take over 2,000 years to reach the world. But if you disciple one person a year and pour God's Word and personal care into that person so thoroughly, then that person disciples another for a year, and you disciple another, and that person disciples another, and no one ever drops the baton, it would only take 34 years to reach the entire world!

> *"Go make disciples."*
> These three words turned the world upside down in the first century.
> They can do it again today.
> These three words turn darkness into light.
> These three words bring hope to the hopeless.
> These three words turn sheep into shepherds.

1) **Ezekiel 34:3-5** - *"You eat the fat and clothe yourselves with the wool, you slaughter the fat sheep without feeding the flock. Those who are sickly you have not strengthened, the diseased you have not healed, the broken you have not bound up, the scattered you have not brought back, nor have you sought for the lost; but with force and with severity you have dominated them. They were scattered for lack of a shepherd, and they became food for every beast of the field and were scattered."*

What is God telling you in this passage?

_____

_____

What blessings is He reminding you of that He has been so good to grant you?

_____

_____

What is He asking you to do?

_____

_____

2) **Ezekiel 34:5** - *"They were scattered for lack of a shepherd, and they became food for every beast of the field and were scattered."*

Describe the flock that He has called you to shepherd.

_____

_____

How does the warning in this verse describe your duty to the flock that has been entrusted to you?

_____

_____

3) **2 Timothy 2:2** - *"The things which you have heard from me in the presence of many witnesses, entrust these to faithful men who will be able to teach others also."*

Who are your "faithful men"?

_____

_____

4) **Ezekiel 34:7-8** - *"Therefore, you shepherds, hear the word of The Lord: 'As I live,' declares The Lord God, 'surely because My flock has become a prey, My flock has even become food for all the beasts of the field for lack of a shepherd, and My shepherds did not search for My flock, but rather the shepherds fed themselves and did not feed My flock.' "*

What happens to the people God asks you to disciple when you don't feed them God's Word?

_____

_____

5) **Ezekiel 34:10** - *"Thus says the Lord God, 'Behold, I am against the shepherds, and I will demand My sheep from them and make them cease from feeding sheep. So the shepherds will not feed themselves anymore, but I will deliver My flock from their mouth, so that they will not be food for them.'"*

Where would your life be without someone who poured into you?

_____

_____

THE SHEPHERD'S CALL

6) **1 Thessalonians 2:8** - *"Having so fond an affection for you, we were well-pleased to impart to you not only the gospel of God but also our own lives, because you had become very dear to us."*

Acts 8:30-32 - *"Philip ran up and heard him (the Ethiopian eunuch) reading Isaiah the prophet, and said, 'Do you understand what you are reading?' And he said, 'Well, how could I, unless someone guides me?' And he invited Philip to come up and sit with him. Now the passage of Scripture which he was reading was this: 'He was led as a sheep to slaughter; and as a lamb before its shearer is silent, so He does not open His mouth.'"*

What are these passages telling you about being a shepherd to your flock?

_____

_____

What two things are required of a true shepherd as he shepherds his flock according to 1 Thessalonians 2:8?

_____

_____

MINUTE OF MEDITATION
"The things which you have heard from me in the presence of many witnesses, entrust these to faithful men who will be able to teach others also"
(2 Timothy 2:2).

PRAYER
Adoration, **C**onfession, **T**hanksgiving, **S**upplication

God Our Protector and Defender

"Who will stand up for me against evildoers? Who will take his stand for me against those who do wickedness? If the Lord had not been my help, my soul would soon have dwelt in the abode of silence" (Psalm 94:16-17).

Psalm 94

The keenly talented veteran quarterback Alex Smith suffered a season-ending injury when the Houston Texans' 288-pound defensive end, J.J. Watt, and 183-pound blitzing cornerback, Kareem Jackson, sacked Smith with 7 minutes 43 seconds left in the third quarter of a November 18, 2018, game. Smith broke both the tibia and fibula of his right leg when all 471 pounds of Watt and Jackson crushed his quaking body.

The injury occurred 33 years to the day after then-Redskins quarterback Joe Theismann suffered a career-ending injury in a game against the New York Giants. Theismann's injury occurred during a Monday night game in 1985.

Theismann's fateful moment happened on a "flea flicker" play as the Giants' linebackers Lawrence Taylor and Harry Carson blitzed and crushed Theismann to the ground. Theismann said it sounded like two muzzled gunshots when his tibia and fibula snapped under the grip of the 240-pound raging body of perhaps the most-feared defenseman in the NFL, Lawrence Taylor. From that point forward, NFL owners began to allot millions of dollars to those who defend the priceless safety of their quarterbacks, the left and right offensive tackles.

The left tackle is often the second-highest-paid player on the team. These 300-pound giants pull in salaries in excess of $10 million per season. The Tennessee Titans recently signed a five-year deal worth $80 million with left tackle Taylor Lewan.

Defending the quarterback of an NFL team costs a team tens of millions of dollars. Defending you and I cost God the life of His Son.

1) **Psalm 94:18** - *"If I should say, 'My foot has slipped,' Your lovingkindness, O Lord, will hold me up."*

   Psalm 17:5 - *"My steps have held fast to Your paths. My feet have not slipped."*

   Psalm 73:2 - *"But as for me, my feet came close to stumbling, my steps had almost slipped."*

   How does Jesus defend you when you fall?
   _____
   _____

   When did your foot slip recently?
   _____
   _____

How did He come to your rescue?

_____
_____

2) **Psalm 94:19** - *"When my anxious thoughts multiply within me, Your consolations delight my soul."*

Psalm 62:6 - *"He only is my rock and my salvation, my stronghold; I shall not be shaken."*

How does Jesus defend you against worry?

_____
_____

What things in your life do you habitually become anxious about?

_____
_____

3) **Psalm 94:22** - *"But the Lord has been my stronghold, and my God the rock of my refuge."*

Deuteronomy 32:4 - *"The Rock! His work is perfect, for all His ways are just; a God of faithfulness and without injustice, righteous and upright is He."*

How does Jesus defend you when you're weak?

_____
_____

Describe a personal weakness with which you need Him the most.

_____
_____

4) **2 Samuel 22:3** - *"My God, my rock, in whom I take refuge, my shield and the horn of my salvation, my stronghold and my refuge; my savior, You save me from violence."*

How does Jesus defend you when you're afraid?

_____
_____

What do you tend to fear?

_____
_____

5) **Romans 8:32-34** - *"He who did not spare His own Son, but delivered Him over for us all, how will He not also with Him freely give us all things? Who will bring a charge against God's elect? God is the one who justifies; who is the one who condemns? Christ Jesus is He who died, yes, rather who was raised, who is at the right hand of God, who also intercedes for us."*

How does Jesus defend your salvation?

_____

_____

When do you doubt God's never-absent, never-tardy, never-ending love? Why?

_____

_____

THE SHEPHERD'S CALL

6) **John 13:15** - *"For I gave you an example that you also should do as I did to you."*

From today's scripture, how does **THE** Shepherd inspire **you** to shepherd **your** flock?

_____

_____

MINUTE OF MEDITATION
"He only is my rock and my salvation, my stronghold; I shall not be shaken"
(Psalm 62:6).

PRAYER
Adoration, **C**onfession, **T**hanksgiving, **S**upplication

Thanksgiving

"For He is our God, and we are the people of His pasture and the sheep of His hand" (Psalm 95:7a).

Psalm 95

Who am I?

I come around once a year. I am an idea with a touch of American history. I am mentioned 114 times in Scripture. My Hebrew name is *Yadah*. My Greek name is *Eucharistia*. I have a holiday named after me. I'm usually associated with pilgrims, turkey, dressing, and cranberry sauce. According to the National Turkey Federation, my holiday will cost 45 million turkeys their lives each year!

I was first celebrated in America in the year 1621. There were about 50 European settlers and around 90 Native Americans who attended the three-day feast. I was declared a legal holiday by President Abraham Lincoln in 1863.

One fine day Jesus healed ten lepers. Only one returned to invoke my name to the One who so graciously saved their lives from shame and rejection.

One out of ten is actually not bad considering that the vast majority of Americans whine about what's wrong with their lives rather than thanking God for their countless blessings! Most Americans talk about the inconsistency of weather conditions far more often than recalling how good God is to us. Just think ... when someone asks how you're doing, you say, "Fine." But to just make you "fine," God has to coordinate in harmonious perfection your 11 organ systems, 206 bones, 656 muscles, the 20,000 breaths that fill your lungs each day, the 115,200 daily beats of your heart, the 100 billion neurons in your brain, the 37.2 trillion cells in your body, etc., etc., etc.

Who am I? You guessed it, *Thanksgiving*!

If you woke up today with only the things you thanked God for yesterday, what would you have to start your day with?

1) **Psalm 95:1-2** - *"O come, let us sing for joy to the Lord, let us shout joyfully to the rock of our salvation. Let us come before His presence with thanksgiving, let us shout joyfully to Him with psalms."*

   When was the last time you "shouted joyfully" to the Lord for your countless blessings?

   _____

   _____

   How often do you give thanks to God compared to the number of times you complain in your thoughts and words? Why?

   _____

   _____

2) **Psalm 95:3-6** - *"For the Lord is a great God and a great King above all gods, in whose hand are the depths of the earth, the peaks of the mountains are His also. The sea is His, for it was He who made it, and His hands formed the dry land. Come, let us worship and bow down, let us kneel before the Lord our Maker."*

Cosmologist Dr. Hugh Ross says the cosmos must be "finely tuned" to the trillion, trillion, trillionth degree of perfection for life to occur on planet earth. Oxford Physicist Dr. Roger Penrose proclaims that the odds of planet earth being found suitable for life are one in ten to the one hundred twenty-eighth power. In short, it is "highly unlikely" that you and I could wake up and say "Good morning" without a divine Creator who was keenly interested in your love and friendship. Try to put into words your gratitude for such miraculous effort and love.

_____

_____

3) **2 Chronicles 5:13** - *"In unison when the trumpeters and the singers were to make themselves heard with one voice to praise and to glorify the Lord, and when they lifted up their voice accompanied by trumpets and cymbals and instruments of music, and when they praised the Lord saying, 'He indeed is good for His lovingkindness is everlasting,' then the house, the house of the Lord, was filled with a cloud."*

Other than using words, how do you express your thanksgiving to God?

_____

_____

4) **2 Corinthians 4:15** - *"For all things are for your sakes, so that the grace which is spreading to more and more people may cause the giving of thanks to abound to the glory of God."*

Describe how the "grace factor" makes you thankful.

_____

_____

5) **2 Corinthians 9:11** - *"You will be enriched in everything for all liberality, which through us is producing thanksgiving to God."*

How does generosity express a thankful heart?

_____

_____

What are some ways (other than money) you can improve your generosity to express your thanksgiving to our benevolent God?

_____

_____

6) **Jeremiah 30:19** - *"From them will proceed thanksgiving and the voice of those who celebrate; and I will multiply them and they will not be diminished; I will also honor them and they will not be insignificant."*

What would your life look like if your heart was filled with thanksgiving 24/7/365?

_____

_____

THE SHEPHERD'S CALL
7) **John 13:15** - *"For I gave you an example that you also should do as I did to you."*

From today's scripture, how does **THE** Shepherd inspire **you** to shepherd **your** flock?

_____

_____

MINUTE OF MEDITATION
"For the Lord is a great God and a great King above all gods, in whose hand are the depths of the earth, the peaks of the mountains are His also. The sea is His, for it was He who made it, and His hands formed the dry land. Come, let us worship and bow down, let us kneel before the Lord our Maker"
(Psalm 95:3-6).

PRAYER
Adoration, **C**onfession, **T**hanksgiving, **S**upplication

A New Song

"Sing to the Lord a new song; sing to the Lord, all the earth" (Psalm 96:1).

Psalm 96

If you scream and yell for your favorite football team, they call you a great fan. If you shout one "hallelujah" in a church, they call you a crazy fanatic. Amazing, isn't it?

There have been an estimated 97 million songs recorded since record-keeping began. The Beatles recorded 305 of those 97 million; Elvis, "the king of rock and roll," recorded 768 of them. But the King of Kings has been the subject of tens of thousands, by far the most prolific song *inspirer* ever. The most-recorded single of all time is "Amazing Grace," written in 1779 by John Newton, a spiritually reborn slave trader. With an estimated 37 million Christian church buildings on earth, the number of hymns and worship songs being sung every service of every day must be uncountable.

Arising from all these statistics is the fact that there are about two new songs recorded every minute. But for a person who loves Jesus, a new song should come out of his or her lips every day. His attributes, His goodness, His grace, and His wisdom are far beyond our ability to fathom.

To get "stuck in a rut" or bored or complacent or disinterested over Jesus is a tribute to a dying or nonexistent faith. To write and sing "a new song" from a heart of love, awe, and gratitude is the mark of a person who is in love with the object of *every* song *ever* written that *eternally* mattered.

1) **Psalm 96:2-3** - *"Sing to the Lord, bless His name; proclaim good tidings of His salvation from day to day. Tell of His glory among the nations, His wonderful deeds among all the peoples."*

   What brings "a new song" to your heart each day?

   _____

   _____

   Is Jesus the subject of your favorite musical meditation? Why or why not?

   _____

   _____

2) **Psalm 96:4-6** - *"For great is the Lord and greatly to be praised; He is to be feared above all gods. For all the gods of the peoples are idols, but the Lord made the heavens. Splendor and majesty are before Him, strength and beauty are in His sanctuary."*

   How can you keep God the song you sing every day?

   _____

   _____

   What negative choices do you make that take God out of your "top hits" each day?

   _____

   _____

3) **Psalm 96:7-8** - *"Ascribe to the Lord, O families of the peoples, ascribe to the Lord glory and strength. Ascribe to the Lord the glory of His name; bring an offering and come into His courts."*

The term *ascribe* comes from the Greek word *apodido*, which means to "regard a quality as belongs to" or "attribute something to a particular person." The synonyms are: *assign, accredit,* or *impute.* What are the attributes of God that you ascribe to Him when you sing to Him "a new song" each day?

_____

_____

4) **Psalm 96:9** - *"Worship the Lord in holy attire; tremble before Him, all the earth."*

How does a believer worship God in "holy attire"?

_____

_____

What does it mean to "tremble before Him" as you worship?

_____

_____

What does an attitude of awe and reverence do to your worship?

_____

_____

To what extent does the mix of rap, country, and rock music in your smartphone contradict the call of Psalm 96?

_____

_____

Why does it matter?

_____

_____

5) **Psalm 96:12-13** - *"Let the field exult, and all that is in it. Then all the trees of the forest will sing for joy before the Lord, for He is coming, for He is coming to judge the earth. He will judge the world in righteousness and the peoples in His faithfulness."*

How should "the coming of the Lord" affect the music of your heart?

_____

_____

THE SHEPHERD'S CALL

6) **John 13:15** - *"For I gave you an example that you also should do as I did to you."*

From today's scripture, how does **THE** Shepherd inspire **you** to shepherd **your** flock?

_____

_____

MINUTE OF MEDITATION

"For great is the Lord and greatly to be praised; He is to be feared above all gods. For all the gods of the peoples are idols, but the Lord made the heavens. Splendor and majesty are before Him, strength and beauty are in His sanctuary" (Psalm 96:4-6).

PRAYER

Adoration, **C**onfession, **T**hanksgiving, **S**upplication

Meekness

"The Lord reigns, let the earth rejoice" (Psalm 97:1a).

Psalm 97

Eternal dominion, unlimited power, and immeasurable strength. Words are not adequate to describe God's omnipotent authority. NASA launched the Wilkinson Microwave Anisotropy Probe satellite in June 2001 and discovered, through never-before-seen universal photographic imaging, with state-of-the-art computer mathematical retro calculations, that at the inception of the cosmos, 100 billion galaxies were thrust more than 1 billion light years in a trillionth of a second.

And yet, while possessing such unfathomable power, God placed Himself in a manger as a tiny baby boy. He touched a helpless leper's grotesquely marred face. He felt the touch of a hemorrhaging woman as a crowd of people pressed in on every side. He placed His fingertips on the eyes of a blind man. He clothed Himself in the meekness of a lamb to be sacrificed on a Roman cross.

Meekness: "power under control." Strength saturated by love. Authority under the submission of mercy. That's the true heart of the Shepherd of all mankind.

1) **Psalm 97:2-3 -** *"Clouds and thick darkness surround Him; righteousness and justice are the foundation of His throne. Fire goes before Him and burns up His adversaries round about."*

   2 Corinthians 5:21 - *"He made Him who knew no sin to be sin on our behalf, so that we might become the righteousness of God in Him."*

   The ultimate paradox: God's unmatched authority, power, and uncompromising righteousness in the heart of One who would succumb to incomprehensible torture and death to bear the burden of His own fury over sin in order to give that righteousness in response to a faithful plea of the most-lowly repentant sinner. Describe in your own words how He did it, why He did it, and your response to His grace clothed in meekness.

   _____

   _____

2) **Psalm 97:4-6 -** *"His lightnings lit up the world; the earth saw and trembled. The mountains melt like wax at the presence of the Lord, at the presence of the Lord of the whole earth. The heavens declare His righteousness, and all the peoples have seen His glory."*
   Name three ways God displays His unlimited power.

   _____

   _____

3) **Psalm 97:7-10** - *"Let all those be ashamed who serve graven images, who boast themselves of idols; worship Him, all you gods. Zion heard this and was glad, and the daughters of Judah have rejoiced because of Your judgments, O Lord. For You are the Lord Most High over all the earth; You are exalted far above all gods. Hate evil, you who love the Lord, Who preserves the souls of His godly ones; He delivers them from the hand of the wicked."*

What should your response be to His power enshrouded in meekness?

_____

_____

How are you doing with that?

_____

_____

4) **Psalm 97:11** - *"Light is sown like seed for the righteous and gladness for the upright in heart."*

When you think about God granting His righteousness to you as a Christ-follower, describe to Him in prayerful journaling the thoughts that enter your mind.

_____

_____

To Him who "sows the seeds of light" into your heart, continue your prayerful journal.

_____

_____

5) **Psalm 97:12** - *"Be glad in the Lord, you righteous ones, and give thanks to His holy name."*

Continue to journal your thoughts as they are stimulated by this passage.

_____

_____

6) **Matthew 5:5** - *"Blessed are the gentle [meek], for they shall inherit the earth."*

What is God asking of you in this passage?

_____

_____

How can you demonstrate meekness to those entrusted to *you* to shepherd?

_____

_____

THE SHEPHERD'S CALL

7) **John 13:15** - *"For I gave you an example that you also should do as I did to you."*

From today's scripture, how does **THE** Shepherd inspire **you** to shepherd **your** flock?

_____

_____

MINUTE OF MEDITATION
"He leads the humble in justice, and He teaches the humble His way"
(Psalm 25:9).

PRAYER
Adoration, **C**onfession, **T**hanksgiving, **S**upplication

The Day of Judgment

"Let the rivers clap their hands, let the mountains sing together for joy before the Lord, for He is coming to judge the earth; He will judge the world with righteousness and the peoples with equity" (Psalm 98:8-9).

Psalm 98

Of the millions of movies, plays, dramas, television scripts, and books that have ever been produced throughout history, there has *never* been one that has captivated the minds and hearts of men and women like the biblical drama of the creation, fall, redemption, judgment, and eternal salvation of mankind. In this drama, we are the actors. The script is divinely inspired. The villain is seemingly unmatched in his power and effectiveness. But the Hero, the Savior, lives and dies in a story that has confounded thoughtful minds for centuries. No greater offer has ever been made. No greater love has ever been shown.

Since the Fall of mankind in the Garden of Eden, men and women have chosen counterfeit love, counterfeit joy, and counterfeit peace. The self-inflicted pain created by these choices has been immeasurable. As the 17th-century French mathematician Blaise Pascal once said, "Apart from Jesus there is only sin, misery, death, despair, and destruction." But the central theme of Scripture is one consistent theme woven throughout the 66 books from "In the beginning" of Genesis 1 to the "Amen" of Revelation 22: God will one day return to the world in the person of the Messiah to bring a final judgment upon the earth and all its inhabitants. At the impending judgment, Christ will grant His pardon to His true followers, and then there will be peace. Then there will be joy; the celebration will be without end.

Perhaps this peace and joy are best described in Revelation 21:1-4: *"Then I saw a new heaven and a new earth; for the first heaven and the first earth passed away, and there is no longer any sea. And I saw the holy city, new Jerusalem, coming down out of heaven from God, made ready as a bride adorned for her husband. And I heard a loud voice from the throne, saying, 'Behold, the tabernacle of God is among men, and He will dwell among them, and they shall be His people, and God Himself will be among them, and He will wipe away every tear from their eyes; and there will no longer be any death; there will no longer be any mourning, or crying, or pain; the first things have passed away.'"*

1) **Psalm 98:1-2** - *"O sing to the Lord a new song, for He has done wonderful things, His right hand and His holy arm have gained the victory for Him. The Lord has made known His salvation; He has revealed His righteousness in the sight of the nations."*

   He *has* done wonderful things, He *has* gained the victory, He *has* made known His salvation, and He *has* revealed His righteousness. Describe in your own words the four acts of God that He has accomplished that bring a new song to your heart.

---

2) **Psalm 98:4-6** - *"Shout joyfully to the Lord, all the earth; break forth and sing for joy and sing praises. Sing praises to the Lord with the lyre, with the lyre and the sound of melody. With trumpets and the sound of the horn shout joyfully before the King, the Lord."*

Describe the extent of the joy and celebration that fills the psalmist's heart (and should fill ours!) as he declares God's ultimate victory as He judges sin and redeems His faithful.

_____

_____

3) **2 Peter 3:9** - *"The Lord is not slow about His promise, as some count slowness, but is patient toward you, not wishing for any to perish but for all to come to repentance."*

1 Timothy 2:3-4 - *"This is good and acceptable in the sight of God our Savior, who desires all men to be saved and to come to the knowledge of the truth."*

As judgment draws near, what is God's final plea to the lost, the stubborn, and the proud?

_____

_____

4) **Romans 2:5** - *"But because of your stubbornness and unrepentant heart you are storing up wrath for yourself in the day of wrath and revelation of the righteous judgment of God."*

1 John 3:3 - *"And everyone who has this hope fixed on Him purifies himself, just as He is pure."*

Compare a hard, unrepentant heart to a soft, repentant heart.

_____

_____

As God examines your heart today, in what way might He see it hard and stubborn? In what way might He see it soft and moldable?

_____

_____

In what ways do you need Him to replace your "heart of stone" with a "heart of flesh" as you anticipate His coming?

_____

_____

5) **Revelation 20:12-15** - *"And I saw the dead, the great and the small, standing before the throne, and books were opened; and another book was opened, which is the book of life; and the dead were judged from the things which were written in the books, according to their deeds. And the sea gave up the dead which were in it, and death and Hades gave up the dead which were in them; and they were judged, every one of them according to their deeds. Then death and Hades were thrown into the lake of fire. This is the second death, the lake of fire. And if anyone's name was not found written in the book of life, he was thrown into the lake of fire."*

Colossians 3:13-14 - *"Bearing with one another, and forgiving each other, whoever has a complaint against anyone; just as the Lord forgave you, so also should you. Beyond all these things put on love, which is the perfect bond of unity."*

Declare your praise for the price Jesus paid for your pardon at the judgment of the nations.

_____

_____

THE SHEPHERD'S CALL

6) **John 13:15** - *"For I gave you an example that you also should do as I did to you."*

From today's scripture, how does **THE** Shepherd inspire **you** to shepherd **your** flock?

_____

_____

MINUTE OF MEDITATION
"The Lord is not slow about His promise, as some count slowness, but is patient toward you, not wishing for any to perish but for all to come to repentance" (2 Peter 3:9).

PRAYER
Adoration, **C**onfession, **T**hanksgiving, **S**upplication

Holy

"The Lord reigns, let the peoples tremble; He is enthroned above the cherubim, let the earth shake! The Lord is great in Zion, and He is exalted above all the peoples. Let them praise Your great and awesome name; Holy is He" (Psalm 99:1-3).

Psalm 99

R.C. Sproul said, "If there is no delight in your soul for the holiness of God, you don't know God. You don't love God. You're out of touch with God. You're asleep to His character."

In John's revelation of the Lamb and the worship He receives in His eternal kingdom, he establishes the standard on which God stands: *"Holy, holy, holy is the Lord God, the Almighty, who was and who is and who is to come"* (Revelation 4:8b).

In so believing, Peter calls the sheep of God's pasture to a relentless pursuit of that very standard He established: *"But like the Holy One who called you, be holy yourselves also in all your behavior"* (1 Peter 1:15).

With a clear understanding that the One who calls us to that standard died on a cross because we're *not* holy, it is only in the *honest pursuit* of that standard that the Christ-follower finds true happiness, peace, intimacy, and fulfillment.

Listen to the words of A.W. Tozer, the highly esteemed 20th-century prophet, minister, and author: "No man should desire to be happy who is not at the same time holy. He should spend his efforts in seeking to know and do the will of God, leaving to Christ the matter of how happy he should be." Charles Spurgeon provides meaningful insight into the accomplishment of that great quest: "If you would be holy, you must live close to Jesus."

1) **Psalm 99:5, 9** - *"Exalt the Lord our God and worship at His footstool; Holy is He. ... Exalt the Lord our God and worship at His holy hill, for holy is the Lord our God."*

Webster's Dictionary offers the synonyms *glorify, extol, praise,* and *acclaim* for the term *exalt*. The Greek term *hupsoo* means "to lift up, raise up, to raise on high." Why does our recognition of God's holiness draw us into praise and exaltation?

_____

_____

2) **Leviticus 20:26** - *"Thus you are to be holy to Me, for I the Lord am holy; and I have set you apart from the peoples to be Mine."*

2 Timothy 2:20-21 - *"Now in a large house there are not only gold and silver vessels, but also vessels of wood and of earthenware, and some to honor and some to dishonor. Therefore, if anyone cleanses himself from these things, he will be a vessel for honor, sanctified, useful to the Master, prepared for every good work."*

In this beautiful word picture from Paul in his last words to Timothy, he echoes the understanding known to all Jews in the early days of God's revelation to His chosen people. To be holy is to be sanctified. To be sanctified is to be set apart. To be set apart is to receive the highest calling in all of life: "to be useful to the Master." What does this calling mean to you?

_____

_____

How do you seize this high calling in your daily walk with Jesus?

_____

_____

Romans 12:2 - *"And do not be conformed to this world, but be transformed by the renewing of your mind, so that you may prove what the will of God is, that which is good and acceptable and perfect."*

In the 21st-century Western world, crazed with social media, entertainment, and chemical stimulants that have distanced us exponentially from biblical living, what standards do you maintain that keep you "set apart" for holy living?

_____

_____

3) **1 Peter 2:9** - *"But you are a chosen race, a royal priesthood, a holy nation, a people for God's own possession, so that you may proclaim the excellencies of Him who has called you out of darkness into His marvelous light."*

What darkness did God call you out of? How does "His marvelous light" feel by comparison? How do you feel toward Him as a result?

_____

_____

4) **1 Corinthians 6:19-20** - *"Or do you not know that your body is a temple of the Holy Spirit who is in you, whom you have from God, and that you are not your own? For you have been bought with a price: therefore glorify God in your body."*

What does Scripture mean when Paul says your body is a "temple of the Holy Spirit"?

_____

_____

How do you personally give proper response to such a calling?

_____

_____

THE SHEPHERD'S CALL

5) **John 13:15** - *"For I gave you an example that you also should do as I did to you."*

From today's scripture, how does **THE** Shepherd inspire **you** to shepherd **your** flock?

_____

_____

MINUTE OF MEDITATION
"And do not be conformed to this world, but be transformed by the renewing of your mind, so that you may prove what the will of God is, that which is good and acceptable and perfect" (Romans 12:2).

PRAYER
Adoration, **C**onfession, **T**hanksgiving, **S**upplication

His!

"Know that the Lord Himself is God; it is He who has made us, and not we ourselves; we are His people and the sheep of His pasture" (Psalm 100:3).

Psalm 100

This entire book and all 150 psalms are wrapped up in this one giant three-letter word: "His!"

I've worked with adopted kids at Kanakuk Kamps for 50 summers, and I've found a most-curious thing about adopted children: Some are exceedingly grateful, some are oblivious, and some are naturally angry toward the parents who have risked the wellbeing of their own families' lives to pull them out of the more-often-than-not dire circumstances from which they were rescued.

As curious as that may be, it's exactly the way it is with those around the world whom God has adopted through the provision of His Son's death.

Sounds crazy, doesn't it? Sadly, those who are either oblivious or angry far outnumber those who are exceedingly grateful.

An earthly adoption often saves a child from a life of neglect or starvation. Heavenly adoption saves a child of God from eternal damnation.

On a 1 to 10 scale, how do you rank yourself in the measurement of appreciation for your adoption? One is angry, three is oblivious, five is thankful, and 10 is exuberant 24/7/365.

If you find yourself anywhere under 10, you would benefit greatly from memorizing and meditating daily on this magnificent Psalm 100.

1) **Romans 8:14-17** - *"For all who are being led by the Spirit of God, these are sons of God. For you have not received a spirit of slavery leading to fear again, but you have received a spirit of adoption as sons by which we cry out, 'Abba! Father!' The Spirit Himself testifies with our spirit that we are children of God, and if children, heirs also, heirs of God and fellow heirs with Christ, if indeed we suffer with Him so that we may also be glorified with Him."*

   "Adopted." "Children of God." "Heirs to the kingdom." How did you rank your heart on the 1 to 10 scale above? How would those around you the most rank your response to God's adoption, measured by the daily joy and appreciation in your life?

   _____

   _____

2) **Psalm 100:1-2** - *"Shout joyfully to the Lord, all the earth. Serve the Lord with gladness; come before Him with joyful singing."*

   What should be the daily attitude of one who truly understands the value of his or her adoption?

   _____

   _____

176

3) **Psalm 100:4 -** *"Enter His gates with thanksgiving and His courts with praise. Give thanks to Him, bless His name."*

In a day when "chill" and "kick back" are standards for daily American life, what is this verse saying to you personally?

_____

_____

4) **Psalm 100:5 -** *"For the Lord is good; His lovingkindness is everlasting and His faithfulness to all generations."*

"Goodness," "everlasting lovingkindness," "faithfulness" --three of God's most-noteworthy attributes! They could be paraphrased this way: "God is always good to His adopted; God is always faithful to His adopted; God is always giving unconditional love to His adopted." How does that truth help set your daily level of joy and appreciation?

_____

_____

5) **John 14:13 -** *"Whatever you ask in My name, that will I do, so that the Father may be glorified in the Son."*

The brilliant 5th-century Algerian writer Augustine once said, "God looks to our profit, not our desire." In other words, He seeks what's best for us, not what we in our limited understanding might want in the moment. In that light, how should you respond when your prayers seem to go unanswered, or even when your prayers are answered contrary to your intention?

_____

_____

6) **Proverbs 3:12 -** *"For whom the Lord loves He reproves, even as a father corrects the son in whom he delights."*

John 15:2 - *"Every branch in Me that does not bear fruit, He takes away; and every branch that bears fruit, He prunes it so that it may bear more fruit."*

Describe a time when God "pruned" or "corrected" you. How did you handle it? What did you think and feel?

_____

_____

7) **Colossians 1:24** - *"Now I rejoice in my sufferings for your sake, and in my flesh I do my share on behalf of His body, which is the church, in filling up what is lacking in Christ's afflictions."*

Philippians 4:4 - *"Rejoice in the Lord always; again I will say, rejoice!"*

What attitude and response adjustments do you need to make during your days of difficulty and discipline?

_____

_____

THE SHEPHERD'S CALL

8) **John 13:15** - *"For I gave you an example that you also should do as I did to you."*

From today's scripture, how does **THE** Shepherd inspire **you** to shepherd **your** flock?

_____

_____

MINUTE OF MEDITATION

"Know that the Lord Himself is God; it is He who has made us, and not we ourselves; we are His people and the sheep of His pasture" (Psalm 100:3).

PRAYER

Adoration, **C**onfession, **T**hanksgiving, **S**upplication

Blameless

"I will give heed to the blameless way. When will You come to me? I will walk within my house in the integrity of my heart. I will set no worthless thing before my eyes; I hate the work of those who fall away; it shall not fasten its grip on me" (Psalm 101:2-3).

Psalm 101

The famous philosopher Yoda (yes, from *Star Wars*) said, "Try not. Do or do not. There is no try." I never aimagined in my wildest dreams that I'd want to quote a *Star Wars* character in a Bible study, but never say never! This is worth a second look, a bit of "Wisdom from the Empire."

I've never liked words like *try, thinking about, wondering if, struggling with,* or any other term that has to do with a lack of heart, a lack of faith, or a lack of commitment. You show me a team that is *trying* to win games and I'll show you a losing team. But take a team that refuses to lose, that "sets its heart on victory," and is willing to work hard enough to prepare for that victory and I'll show you a winner.

When I meet a man who is "struggling with a sin" or "trying" to stop an addictive habit, I'm positive he'll be back at it when he has a moment of weakness or a moment of loneliness, sadness, or anger. But I meet men and women every day who once were living in sin, but they *set their hearts* to quit, and now they celebrate a day of victory with every setting of the sun.

Psalm 101:3 is one of those Bible verses that "winning" coaches are eternally attracted to. *"I will set no worthless thing before my eyes"* is the kind of thinking that puts the ball across the goal line. It's the kind of purposefulness that takes teams to the locker room shouting in victory! It's the kind of intentionality that takes a believer along the pathway of blamelessness on which all true believers have been called to live.

1) **Philippians 3:16** - *"However, let us keep living by that same standard to which we have attained."*

   If Jesus *made* us "blameless" on the day He was crucified, *established* our blamelessness on the day we placed our faith in Him, and *called* us to love blamelessly every day of our lives, what importance should we place on living that way?

   _____

   _____

2) **Daniel 1:8** - *"But Daniel made up his mind that he would not defile himself with the king's choice food or with the wine which he drank; so he sought permission from the commander of the officials that he might not defile himself."*

   How did Daniel's decision to "purpose his heart" to live by God's standards result in great blessing and honor?

   _____

   _____

3) **1 Peter 2:9-12** - *"But you are a chosen race, a royal priesthood, a holy nation, a people for God's own possession, so that you may proclaim the excellencies of Him who has called you out of darkness into His marvelous light; for you once were not a people, but now you are the people of God; you had not received mercy, but now you have received mercy. Beloved, I urge you as aliens and strangers to abstain from fleshly lusts which wage war against the soul. Keep your behavior excellent among the Gentiles, so that in the thing in which they slander you as evildoers, they may because of your good deeds, as they observe them, glorify God in the day of visitation."*

How does your "high calling" from God motivate you to *purpose your heart* to godly living?

_____

_____

4) **Ephesians 2:10** - *"For we are His workmanship, created in Christ Jesus for good works, which God prepared beforehand so that we would walk in them."*

How does a commitment to "live by purpose" in pursuit of the good works prepared for us compare to "going with the flow"?

_____

_____

5) **Psalm 37:5-6** - *"Commit your way to the Lord, trust also in Him, and He will do it. He will bring forth your righteousness as the light and your judgment as the noonday."*

What do these verses suggest God will do in response to our commitment to live by purpose for Him?

_____

_____

6) **1 Kings 8:61** - *"Let your heart therefore be wholly devoted to the Lord our God, to walk in His statutes and to keep His commandments, as at this day."*

In what ways do you tend to justify, rationalize, cop out, and otherwise fail to walk fully committed to Christ?

_____

_____

How do you believe God is calling you to live differently today?

_____

_____

THE SHEPHERD'S CALL

7) **John 13:15** - *"For I gave you an example that you also should do as I did to you."*

From today's scripture, how does **THE** Shepherd inspire **you** to shepherd **your** flock?

_____

_____

MINUTE OF MEDITATION

"For we are His workmanship, created in Christ Jesus for good works, which God prepared beforehand so that we would walk in them" (Ephesians 2:10).

PRAYER

Adoration, **C**onfession, **T**hanksgiving, **S**upplication

The Lamb in Distress

"For my days have been consumed in smoke, and my bones have been scorched like a hearth. My heart has been smitten like grass and has withered away, indeed, I forget to eat my bread" (Psalm 102:3-4).

Psalm 102

I had heard stories about heart attacks--how your chest tightens, how a sharp pain would seize the left side of your chest, how the underside of your arms would grow numb and tingle. But until it happens to you, you can't fully understand the overarching mental and emotional drama that overtakes you. Death stares you in the face, and your life flashes before your eyes.

My reaction to my first heart attack wasn't what you'd call stereotypical. Stemming from my training in "mental toughness" through years of junior high, high school, and college football, I tried to push my three "mild," successive heart attacks aside and ignore the reality of what I knew to be true. Fortunately, they weren't enough to throw me to the ground or take my life.

The open heart surgery was an experience of anguish and pain like this boy had never known before. Having a vein stripped out of the full length of my leg, my chest cracked open, and tubes inserted in my abdomen all worked together to bring a new level of intensity to days and nights of pain and sleeplessness. Surprisingly, my lung cavities filled with blood and suffocated my ability to breath. Another emergency surgery, through the ribs of my back, added two more weeks to the desperation. Five tubes and 28 sleepless days and nights later, I wept tears of joy as the final tubes were removed and I was released from the hospital to begin a long road of recovery.

I've never been so thankful to leave a place in my life! I'll never cease thanking God for the ability to walk again, breathe again, and enjoy life as I do today. Though filled with painful procedures and physical agony, the hospital stay was an experience of closeness to God and silent worship like I've never known. My hospital room was a sanctuary. God kept me awake so I could experience His love fully. He extended my stay so I could more deeply experience His peace. The grass in His pasture is greenest when the sky opens and heavy rain falls to the earth.

1) **Psalm 102:1-2** - *"Hear my prayer, O Lord! And let my cry for help come to You. Do not hide Your face from me in the day of my distress; incline Your ear to me; in the day when I call answer me quickly."*

Describe the day in your life when the clouds were the deepest gray, the pain was the most intense, and the lightning crashed to the earth. If you could have written out your prayers that day, what would they have said?

_____

_____

2) **John 15:1-2** - *"I am the true vine, and My Father is the vinedresser. Every branch in Me that does not bear fruit, He takes away; and every branch that bears fruit, He prunes it so that it may bear more fruit."* What is God's principle for "pruning" a Christ-follower?

_____

_____

3) **2 Corinthians 1:3-5** - *"Blessed be the God and Father of our Lord Jesus Christ, The Father of mercies and God of all comfort, who comforts us in all our affliction so that we will be able to comfort those who are in any affliction with the comfort with which we ourselves are comforted by God. For just as the sufferings of Christ are ours in abundance, so also our comfort is abundant through Christ."*

The Greek word for *comfort* is *paraklete*, which means "encouragement, consolation, to call or beseech." In Barclay's commentary, he compares the term *comfort* to a general who "speaks a word of bravery" to a defeated army, giving a word of motivation to take his soldiers back into battle. How have you seen God use your afflictions to enable you to "speak a word of bravery" to someone who is going through the same brokenness you've experienced?

_____

_____

Why is it necessary to be broken in order to fully lift up another in his or her brokenness?

_____

_____

4) **Psalm 147:3** - *"He heals the brokenhearted and binds up their wounds."*

It has been said that God gives us 20/20 vision looking backward to see His hand in everything. How have you experienced God's healing in your brokenness?

_____

_____

5) **Psalm 51:16-17** - *"For You do not delight in sacrifice, otherwise I would give it; You are not pleased with burnt offering. The sacrifices of God are a broken spirit; a broken and a contrite heart, O God, You will not despise."*

Why does a humble, broken spirit bring God's blessing to a believer?

_____

_____

THE SHEPHERD'S CALL

6) **John 13:15** - *"For I gave you an example that you also should do as I did to you."*

From today's scripture, how does **THE** Shepherd inspire **you** to shepherd **your** flock?

_____

_____

MINUTE OF MEDITATION

"Blessed be the God and Father of our Lord Jesus Christ, the Father of mercies and God of all comfort, who comforts us in all our affliction so that we will be able to comfort those who are in any affliction with the comfort with which we ourselves are comforted by God. For just as the sufferings of Christ are ours in abundance, so also our comfort is abundant through Christ"
(2 Corinthians 1:3-5).

PRAYER

Adoration, **C**onfession, **T**hanksgiving, **S**upplication

The Goodness of God

"I [Jesus] am the good shepherd; the good shepherd lays down His life for the sheep" (John 10:11).

Psalm 103

Shortly after I was diagnosed with leukemia, I was getting a blood profile drawn by my oncologist in Memphis. That particular day, I had a bad case of the blues. I was worried, afraid, and ... well, I hate needles in my arms!

My nurse was an elderly, church-going woman who had grown up in the impoverished Deep South and embodied all the goodness one person could possess. Her mannerisms were gentle, joyful, and kind. As I sat down and extended my arm for yet one more blood draw, my emotions got the best of me.

The nurse said with the tender voice of an angel, "How you doin'?"

I said past the lump of sadness in my throat, "God is good."

She gently looked me in the eyes and, with her beautiful, aged, brown eyes, speaking in the sweetness of honey, responded, "All the time. AAAAALLL the time, God is good."

It might as well have been an angel, and perhaps she was one. My heart relaxed, and my worries melted away. I knew it in my head, but that dear lady helped that blessed thought shift resolutely into my heart. God is good all the time. All the time, God is good.

Psalm 103 offers the same reassurance. Read it in its entirety. Read it slowly, and meditate on each verse. It's well worth your time to memorize and meditate on it daily. It's better at night, when you put your head on your pillow after a hard day, than any sleeping pill ever prescribed. (I know. I've meditated on it hundreds of nights myself after a shattering day of pressure, stress, and pain.)

1) **Psalm 103:1-2** - *"Bless the Lord, O my soul, and all that is within me, bless His holy name. Bless the Lord, O my soul, and forget none of His benefits."*

   Why is it important for the deepening of your relationship with God to remember all the goodness He has brought you since the day you took your first breath on this earth?

   _____

   _____

2) **Psalm 103:5** - *"Who satisfies your years with good things, so that your youth is renewed like the eagle."*

While God has blessed medical doctors with great knowledge and skills, no doctor can ever take credit for healing anyone. Doctors can partner with God and facilitate a better healing process, but any faith-filled physician will gladly tell you that the credit belongs to God. Likewise, only a sovereign God who placed His Son on a Roman cross can forgive sins. Why does a conscious recognition of those truths "renew your youth like the eagle"?

_____

_____

3) **Psalm 103:8-9** - *"The Lord is compassionate and gracious, slow to anger and abounding in lovingkindness. He will not always strive with us, nor will He keep His anger forever."*

Express in a few words your thankfulness for God's graciousness, compassion, patience, and lovingkindness.

_____

_____

4) **Psalm 103:10-12** - *"He has not dealt with us according to our sins, nor rewarded us according to our iniquities. For as high as the heavens are above the earth, so great is His lovingkindness toward those who fear Him. As far as the east is from the west, so far has He removed our transgressions from us."*

Grace = getting what we *don't* deserve. Mercy = not getting what we *do* deserve.

What is God saying to you personally in these verses?

_____

_____

5) **Psalm 103:13** - *"Just as a father has compassion on his children, so the Lord has compassion on those who fear Him."*

A good dad will give it all for his children. What a great metaphor! What does this promise mean to you?

_____

_____

6) **Psalm 103:15-18** - *"As for man, his days are like grass; as a flower of the field, so he flourishes. When the wind has passed over it, it is no more, and its place acknowledges it no longer. But the lovingkindness of the Lord is from everlasting to everlasting on those who fear Him, and His righteousness to children's children, to those who keep His covenant and remember His precepts to do them."*

If indeed eternity is forever and 100 years of life on earth are but a speck of sand on an ocean beach, what does that say about the importance of obeying God as we're exhorted in this passage?

_____

_____

THE SHEPHERD'S CALL

7) **John 13:15** - *"For I gave you an example that you also should do as I did to you."*

From today's scripture, how does **THE** Shepherd inspire **you** to shepherd **your** flock?

_____

_____

MINUTE OF MEDITATION

"He has not dealt with us according to our sins, nor rewarded us according to our iniquities. For as high as the heavens are above the earth, so great is His lovingkindness toward those who fear Him. As far as the east is from the west, so far has He removed our transgressions from us" (Psalm 103:10-12).

PRAYER
Adoration, **C**onfession, **T**hanksgiving, **S**upplication

God of Wonder

"Bless the Lord, O my soul! O Lord my God, You are very great; You are clothed with splendor and majesty, covering Yourself with light as with a cloak, stretching out heaven like a tent curtain" (Psalm 104:1-2).

Psalm 104

How did the cosmos form? How did it begin? Was it always there, the "eternal constant," as Darwin surmised? What about the mystery of the four seasons of the year? What causes the earth to annually and predictably adjust from summer to spring to fall to winter? Was there a worldwide flood? If so, what happened to all the water that covered the tallest mountains by 15 cubits? Where did the water go? How did the water dissipate in just half a year?

If I told you that the psalmist, writing in about 1,000 BC, knew the scientific answers to all the above and wrote them all in one psalm, would you be surprised? Would you believe in divine inspiration?

"Covering Yourself with light as with a cloak, stretching out heaven like a tent curtain" (Psalm 104:2).

"It is He who sits above the circle of the earth, and its inhabitants are like grasshoppers, Who stretches out the heavens like a curtain and spreads them out like a tent to dwell in" (Isaiah 40:22).

Recent data from NASA, published on April 8, 2017, established the fact that the cosmos indeed had a beginning. From the moment of supernatural inception, it expanded "like a giant curtain being drawn across the heavens," a trillion trillion-fold in the first trillionth of a trillionth of a second.

Indeed, an all-powerful being stretched the giant curtain instantly across the heavens to defy all laws of naturalistic science.

"He established the earth upon its foundations, so that it will not totter forever and ever. You covered it with the deep as with a garment; the waters were standing above the mountains. At Your rebuke they fled, at the sound of Your thunder they hurried away. The mountains rose; the valleys sank down *to the place which You established for them"* (Psalm 104:5-8, emphasis added).

With countless fossil deposits all over the earth and under the earth, from tiny bacteria to 80-foot-long dinosaur skeletons, all buried instantly under layers of mud, sand, and gravel in a cataclysmic, worldwide flood-- the evidence of such a flood exists on all seven continents. Some sea-going fossils have even been discovered as high as 29,029 feet above sea level in the Himalayan mountains (i.e., near the summit of Everest). There is only naive doubt that the flood is factual and historical. Furthermore, a National Geographic study published on September 13, 2000, produced evidence of a several-thousand-year-old human habitation 300 feet *below* the surface of the Black Sea 12 miles off the Turkish coast.

192

Coupled with the evidence of *vertical* and semi-vertical layers of hardened sediment in the geology of the giant Rocky Mountains, the Himalayan Mountains, and the Apennine Mountains, as well as the deep sedimentary-layered canyons in Arizona, Peru, Australia, and Namibia, the evidence bears witness to an instant raising of the mountains and the lowering of the seas at the end of the flood, causing the waters to rush through the hardened layers of mud, sand, and gravel in the valleys below.

"He made the moon for the seasons; the sun knows the place of its setting" (Psalm 104:19).

Finally, the moon is credited with two-thirds of the "precision effect" of the 23.4-degree tilt of the earth's axis. It is the critical, exact tilt of the earth's axis that causes the four seasons vital to the production of crops that feed our hungry planet. Twenty-five hundred years before Copernicus correctly positioned the moon as a satellite of the earth in the earth's rotation around the sun, how did the psalmist know the secret of the "precision effect" and the moon's influence on the seasons?

Surely the psalmist had the divinely inspired news release many centuries before science even had a clue.

1) **Psalm 104:1-24** - *"Bless the Lord, O my soul! O Lord my God, You are very great; You are clothed with splendor and majesty. ... O Lord, how many are Your works! In wisdom You have made them all; the earth is full of Your possessions."*

   Does the greatness of God increase your awe of and reverence for Him? How does it affect your worship of the Creator?

   _____

   _____

2) **Romans 1:19-20** - *"Because that which is known about God is evident within them; for God made it evident to them. For since the creation of the world His invisible attributes, His eternal power and divine nature, have been clearly seen, being understood through what has been made, so that they are without excuse."*

   What is Scripture saying about humanism, naturalism, and atheism?

   _____

   _____

3) **2 Timothy 1:9** - *"Who has saved us and called us with a holy calling, not according to our works, but according to His own purpose and grace which was granted us in Christ Jesus from all eternity."*

Titus 1:2 - *"In the hope of eternal life, which God, who cannot lie, promised long ages ago."*

The work of astrophysicists Stephen Hawking, Jane Hawking, and Don Page proved that time was also created. Astrophysicist Dr. Hugh Ross stated on April 16, 1994, "If you prove time had a beginning, that it was created, it eliminates all theological positions but Jesus Christ." What does such coordination of Scripture and science tell you about God and the Bible?

---

4) **Psalm 147:5** - *"Great is our Lord and abundant in strength; His understanding is infinite."*

1 Corinthians 1:25 - *"Because the foolishness of God is wiser than men, and the weakness of God is stronger than men."*

Hugh Ross also stated that in terms of the gravitational constant of the cosmos alone, God must be 100 trillion trillion times more precise than man. (That's just *1* of 41 fine-tuned characteristics necessary to have a planet that supports life as we know it on earth! If all 41 factors were included, there would not be enough space on the page to print all the zeros in the measure of God's "fine tuning" precision.) How does that incredible wisdom of God affect your view of Him? Does it make you want to draw closer to His shepherd's heart in wonder and awe?

---

5) **Jeremiah 10:6** - *"There is none like You, O Lord; You are great, and great is Your name in might."*

1 Chronicles 16:25 - *"For great is the Lord, and greatly to be praised; He also is to be feared above all gods."*

The visible size of the universe is 93 billion light years in diameter, encompassing more than 100 billion galaxies with at least 100 billion stars in each galaxy. But that's only what we can observe. No one knows the vastness of our starry "home." Describe the "God of Wonder" in your own words.

---

6) **1 Chronicles 29:11 -** *"Yours, O Lord, is the greatness and the power and the glory and the victory and the majesty, indeed everything that is in the heavens and the earth; Yours is the dominion, O Lord, and You exalt Yourself as head over all."*

Why is it futile, pointless, and intellectually impossible to put God in a "man-sized box"?

    a. In your personal worldview?

_____

_____

    b. With a challenge you're facing in your life today?

_____

_____

THE SHEPHERD'S CALL

7) **John 13:15 -** *"For I gave you an example that you also should do as I did to you."*

From today's scripture, how does **THE** Shepherd inspire **you** to shepherd **your** flock?

_____

_____

MINUTE OF MEDITATION

"O Lord, how many are Your works! In wisdom You have made them all; the earth is full of Your possessions" (Psalm 104:24).

PRAYER

Adoration, **C**onfession, **T**hanksgiving, **S**upplication

The Faithful Shepherd

"Seek the Lord and His strength; seek His face continually. Remember His wonders which He has done, His marvels and the judgments uttered by His mouth" (Psalm 105:4-5).

Psalm 105

God shows us the future to prepare our hearts. He shows us the present to guard our hearts. He shows us the past to remind our hearts of His reliable love and unwavering faithfulness.

When God makes a covenant, He seals it in blood. When God gives a promise, He stakes the life of His Son on that promise.

History testifies to the day God made a covenant with Abraham that "the land of the Canaanites" would always belong to His people, the Hebrew nation. Much like the timing of the promises He makes you and me today, the Jews were unaware of God's *greater plan* in fulfilling that promise. As an old Southern Baptist preacher testified one Sunday morning in his small, rural church, "God may not get there when you want Him to, but He'll be there right on time."

Psalm 105 is a great historical remembrance of the flight of Joseph and the 400-year plight of God's people in Egyptian bondage. As God disciplined and cleansed His people and subsequently demonstrated His mighty wonders in the Jews' "liberation drama," He brought His people back to their land. A second exile of 70 years began in 605 BC, and a third diaspora of 1,900 years started in AD 67. Then, against all odds, Israel militarily reclaimed its land in 1948. Today, the sovereign nation remains one of the top five most-powerful countries in the world.

1) **Psalm 105:1-3** - *"Oh give thanks to the Lord, call upon His name; make known His deeds among the peoples. Sing to Him, sing praises to Him; speak of all His wonders. Glory in His holy name; let the heart of those who seek the Lord be glad."*

   When you look back over your life and see God's hand in your provision and benefits, how do these remembrances affect your worship and praise of Him?

   _____

   _____

2) **Psalm 105:8-11** - *"He has remembered His covenant forever, the word which He commanded to a thousand generations, the covenant which He made with Abraham, and His oath to Isaac. Then He confirmed it to Jacob for a statute, to Israel as an everlasting covenant, saying, 'To you I will give the land of Canaan as the portion of your inheritance.'"*

   On May 14, 1948, using the United Nations, God gave His people back their homeland after almost 2,000 years of being dispersed around the world. But the seven Arab nations that surrounded them set out to destroy the new, feeble nation. Yet the nation of Israel maintained its statehood and continues to strengthen it to this day.

   What does the Abrahamic covenant and God's fulfillment of it in the great mystery of Israel's existence say to you about the promises God has made about your past sins forgiven and your hope for eternal life?

   _____

   _____

3) **Psalm 105:17-23** - *"He sent a man before them, Joseph, who was sold as a slave. They afflicted his feet with fetters, he himself was laid in irons; until the time that his word came to pass, the word of the Lord tested him. The king sent and released him, the ruler of peoples, and set him free. He made him lord of his house and ruler over all his possessions, to imprison his princes at will, that he might teach his elders wisdom. Israel also came into Egypt; thus Jacob sojourned in the land of Ham."*

   How can you relate to Joseph? When were you in bondage? How did God set you free? How did He show you His wonders in the process?

   _____

   _____

4) **Psalm 106:6-8** - *"We have sinned like our fathers, we have committed iniquity, we have behaved wickedly. Our fathers in Egypt did not understand Your wonders; they did not remember Your abundant kindnesses, but rebelled by the sea, at the Red Sea. Nevertheless He saved them for the sake of His name, that He might make His power known."*

   How have you mimicked the Jews when God was not on your timetable in your challenges and trials?

   _____

   _____

5) **2 Timothy 2:13** - *"If we are faithless, He remains faithful, for He cannot deny Himself."*

How do you respond when God's faithfulness becomes evident in your present, your future, and your past?

_____

_____

How can your faith improve in light of God's unwavering faithfulness?

_____

_____

THE SHEPHERD'S CALL

6) **John 13:15** - *"For I gave you an example that you also should do as I did to you."*

From today's scripture, how does **THE** Shepherd inspire **you** to shepherd **your** flock?

_____

_____

MINUTE OF MEDITATION
"Seek the Lord and His strength; seek His face continually. Remember His wonders which He has done, His marvels and the judgments uttered by His mouth" (Psalm 105:4-5).

PRAYER
Adoration, **C**onfession, **T**hanksgiving, **S**upplication

The Redeeming Shepherd

"Oh give thanks to the Lord, for He is good, for His lovingkindness is everlasting. Let the redeemed of the Lord say so, whom He has redeemed from the hand of the adversary" (Psalm 107:1-2).

Psalm 107

Just like a picture window on the eastern wall of a beautiful living room, fully opened to the morning sunrise, countless rays of sunlight penetrate every room, lifting the cold shadows of night from the house... the Greek term *exagoridzo* ("redemption") means "to be bought out of the slave market, never to go back into slavery again!"

"In Him we have redemption through His blood, the forgiveness of our trespasses, according to the riches of His grace which He lavished on us. In all wisdom and insight ..." (Ephesians 1:7-8).

In Jesus, we have been bought out of the slave market of addiction, worldly allurements, detrimental relationships, worry, guilt, shame, and bitterness--ALL put to rest forever under the blood of His crucified body. *"Tetelestai!"* He cried on the cross. "It is finished." Not *He* is finished, but our slavery is finished. Our guilt and shame are finished. Our fear of death is finished. Satan's grip of sin upon our hearts has been released.

"When you were dead in your transgressions and the uncircumcision of your flesh, He made you alive together with Him, having forgiven us all our transgressions, having canceled out the certificate of debt consisting of decrees against us, which was hostile to us; and He has taken it out of the way, having nailed it to the cross" (Colossians 2:13-14).

Our certificate of debt is paid in full. Our redemption has been accomplished in Christ's horrific sacrifice on the cross. Your very soul, your eternal life, has been purchased from the market of slavery and condemnation, never to return into bondage again.

1) **Psalm 107:8-9** - *"Let them give thanks to the Lord for His lovingkindness, and for His wonders to the sons of men! For He has satisfied the thirsty soul, and the hungry soul He has filled with what is good."*

   Give thanksgiving as you recount three of your most-cherished memories of times that God has redeemed your past challenges and valleys of darkness.

   _____

   _____

2) **Psalm 107:21-22** - *"Let them give thanks to the Lord for His lovingkindness, and for His wonders to the sons of men! Let them also offer sacrifices of thanksgiving, and tell of His works with joyful singing."*

How should your thoughts and words of thanksgiving for God's redeeming grace cleanse your soul and clear a pathway for godly living?

_____

_____

3) **Romans 8:31, 37-39** - *"What then shall we say to these things? If God is for us, who is against us?... But in all these things we overwhelmingly conquer through Him who loved us. For I am convinced that neither death, nor life, nor angels, nor principalities, nor things present, nor things to come, nor powers, nor height, nor depth, nor any other created thing, will be able to separate us from the love of God, which is in Christ Jesus our Lord."*

As Paul's reassuring words encapsulate our redemption, describe the joy and thanksgiving that fill your heart, mind, and soul.

_____

_____

4) **Romans 3:24** - *"... being justified as a gift by His grace through the redemption which is in Christ Jesus."*

Luke 21:4 - *"... for they all out of their surplus put into the offering; but she out of her poverty put in all that she had to live on."*

We sing our choruses: "He paid it all!" "He loves me so." "He is faithful." "Oh, how He loves you and me." "He paid my debt." "He left the 99 to come find me." These and countless others praise His all-out, sold out, unconditional love. What song might the widow have been singing to Jesus in the Luke 21 account of her all-out gift?

_____

_____

Why does the widow's song ring so sweetly in Jesus' ears?

_____

_____

Why does His all-out love demand our all-out love in response?

_____

_____

What song are you singing today in your heart's meditations, the way you entertain yourself, the words from your mouth, and the portion of your time and money you give to the needy and less fortunate?

_____

_____

THE SHEPHERD'S CALL

5) **John 13:15** - *"For I gave you an example that you also should do as I did to you."*

From today's scripture, how does **THE** Shepherd inspire **you** to shepherd **your** flock?

_____

_____

MINUTE OF MEDITATION

"Oh give thanks to the Lord, for He is good, for His lovingkindness is everlasting. Let the redeemed of the Lord say so, whom He has redeemed from the hand of the adversary" (Psalm 107:1-2).

PRAYER

Adoration, **C**onfession, **T**hanksgiving, **S**upplication

Steadfastness

"My heart is steadfast, O God; I will sing, I will sing praises, even with my soul. Awake, harp and lyre; I will awaken the dawn! I will give thanks to You, O Lord, among the peoples, and I will sing praises to You among the nations. For Your lovingkindness is great above the heavens, and Your truth reaches to the skies. Be exalted, O God, above the heavens, and Your glory above all the earth" (Psalm 108:1-5).

Psalm 108

The sun is 864,938 miles in diameter and shines upon the earth from its solar perch approximately 92,955,807 miles away. Every square inch of the sun exudes over 300,000 candlepower of light, burning at a temperature of about 10,000 degrees Fahrenheit. Our planet is adequately warmed by absorbing one billionth of the sun's remarkable power.

Yet, the sun is but a baby star in the cosmic expanse that surrounds us. There are more than 10 septillion (10 followed by 24 zeros) active stars in our known cosmos. Most of them dwarf the sun in power and magnitude. Polaris (the North Star of the Little Dipper star group) is 1,600 times more luminous than the sun. Deneb (in the Cygnus star group) is 196,000 times more luminous than the sun. But the most luminous of all is the Star R136 that maintains 8,700,000 times as much power as our sun.

Oh, the power of God!

To travel to our nearest neighbor, Mars, would require a vacation planner 571,000 hours if you were to obey the 70 m.p.h. speed limit of the American interstate highway. But if you speed up your space traveler to the speed of light (600 million, million m.p.h.), you could reach the sun in 1 light year, Polaris in 323 light years, and Deneb in 2,616 light years. At such a speed you could reach our nearest neighboring galaxy, Sagittarius Dwarf Elliptical, in 179,000 light years, and the picturesque Whirlpool Galaxy in 23.16 million light years. But it would take a staggering 13.4 billion light years to travel to GN-z11 Galaxy in the outer banks of our known cosmos. Many scientists believe we have only a tiny glimpse of that which lies beyond what our most-powerful telescopes can interpret.

Oh, the bigness of God!

And to think that the power of God and the bigness of God are only a small snapshot of all His attributes of majesty and splendor!

Beyond existence lies truth. Beyond truth lies knowledge. Beyond knowledge lies wisdom. Beyond wisdom lies relationship. Beyond relationship lies love. Beyond love lie awe, majesty, and wonder. Beyond wonder lies praise. Beyond praise lies worship. But the beauty of knowing and walking with God is this, "Beyond worship is *steadfastness*, the ultimate expression of admiration and love."

1) **Lamentations 3:22-23** - *"The Lord's lovingkindnesses indeed never cease, for His compassions never fail. They are new every morning; great is Your faithfulness."*

The Greek term *hedraios* translates to "sitting, steadfast." Webster's dictionary defines the term *steadfast* as "firm in belief, determination, or allegiance." The synonym is *faithful*. Describe a heart that is *steadfast* for God.

_____

_____

2) **Job 19:17-27** - *"My breath is offensive to my wife, and I am loathsome to my own brothers. Even young children despise me; I rise up and they speak against me. All my associates abhor me, and those I love have turned against me. My bone clings to my skin and my flesh, and I have escaped only by the skin of my teeth. Pity me, pity me, O you my friends, for the hand of God has struck me. Why do you persecute me as God does, and are not satisfied with my flesh? Oh that my words were written! Oh that they were inscribed in a book! That with an iron stylus and lead they were engraved in the rock forever! As for me, I know that my Redeemer lives, and at the last He will take His stand on the earth. Even after my skin is destroyed, yet from my flesh I shall see God; whom I myself shall behold, and whom my eyes will see and not another. My heart faints within me!"*

With this reminder of Job's steadfast heart, whom do *you* admire the most in terms of a steadfast heart? Why?

_____

_____

3) **1 Peter 5:2-3** - *"Shepherd the flock of God among you, exercising oversight not under compulsion, but voluntarily, according to the will of God; and not for sordid gain, but with eagerness; nor yet as lording it over those allotted to your charge, but proving to be examples to the flock."*

Titus 1:7-8 - *"For the overseer must be above reproach as God's steward, not self-willed, not quick-tempered, not addicted to wine, not pugnacious, not fond of sordid gain, but hospitable, loving what is good, sensible, just, devout, self-controlled."*

Describe the steadfast heart that's demanded of one who is called to be a 'shepherd of the flock" and to pour the love of God into the heart of another.

_____

_____

4) **2 Timothy 3:14-15** - *"You, however, continue in the things you have learned and become convinced of, knowing from whom you have learned them, and that from childhood you have known the sacred writings which are able to give you the wisdom that leads to salvation through faith which is in Christ Jesus."*

   Jude 1:24-25 - *"Now to Him who is able to keep you from stumbling, and to make you stand in the presence of His glory blameless with great joy, to the only God our Savior, through Jesus Christ our Lord, be glory, majesty, dominion and authority, before all time and now and forever. Amen."*

   How is the deepening of your love and admiration for God's steadfastness through the study of His Word causing you to grow in your steadfast love for, and commitment toward, Him?

   _____

   _____

5) **Jude 1:20-21** - *"But you, beloved, building yourselves up on your most holy faith, praying in the Holy Spirit, keep yourselves in the love of God, waiting anxiously for the mercy of our Lord Jesus Christ to eternal life."*

   1 Peter 4:1-2 - *"Therefore, since Christ has suffered in the flesh, arm yourselves also with the same purpose, because he who has suffered in the flesh has ceased from sin, so as to live the rest of the time in the flesh no longer for the lusts of men, but for the will of God."*

   What is an area at the core of your heart where you long for *your* steadfastness to grow?

   _____

   _____

6) **Colossians 3:5-10** - *"Therefore consider the members of your earthly body as dead to immorality, impurity, passion, evil desire, and greed, which amounts to idolatry. For it is because of these things that the wrath of God will come upon the sons of disobedience, and in them you also once walked, when you were living in them. But now you also, put them all aside: anger, wrath, malice, slander, and abusive speech from your mouth. Do not lie to one another, since you laid aside the old self with its evil practices, and have put on the new self who is being renewed to a true knowledge according to the image of the One who created him."*

   How is God speaking to you today in terms of putting on "the new self": immoveable, unshakable, unwavering, and steadfast of heart?

   _____

   _____

THE SHEPHERD'S CALL

7) **John 13:15** - *"For I gave you an example that you also should do as I did to you."*

From today's scripture, how does **THE** Shepherd inspire **you** to shepherd **your** flock?

_____

_____

MINUTE OF MEDITATION

"Shepherd the flock of God among you, exercising oversight not under compulsion, but voluntarily, according to the will of God; and not for sordid gain, but with eagerness; nor yet as lording it over those allotted to your charge, but proving to be examples to the flock" (1 Peter 5:2-3).

PRAYER

Adoration, Confession, Thanksgiving, Supplication

Take Them to Glory

"The Lord says to my Lord: 'Sit at My right hand until I make Your enemies a footstool for Your feet'" (Psalm 110:1).

Psalm 110

Flying 32,000 feet above the Pacific Ocean tonight on a five-and-a-half-hour hop to "The Garden Island" of the Pacific, Kauai, to take my grandkids scuba diving in the warm and picturesque Hawaiian waters fills this old grandpa with happiness and anticipation in indescribable proportions. Leading children in scuba diving experiences in the vast underwater aquarium of our life has long been one of my greatest thrills.

But then, to lead my grandkids spelunking with only a flashlight into a wilderness crystal cave, squeezing through tiny limestone passageways into scarcely seen rooms filled with treasure chests of trillions of tiny gypsum and calcite crystals, rivals the adventures under the sea in every conceivable manner.

Yes, guiding kids on river trips, fishing trips, hunting trips, flying adventures, and mission trips to experience the joy of amazement, of living, of laughing, of loving, and of giving is, to me, the ten-carat diamond in the sand of life.

But none of these extravagant guiding adventures compares to the greatest adventure of all, taking a student trip to "the Heart of the Shepherd."

David, king of Israel, in all his splendor, in all his glory, somehow knew in his divinely inspired thinking that up there, out there, over there, somewhere, was the Messiah, sitting at the right hand of God. And in his wonderful Psalms, he takes us there so we can join him in this, the greatest guiding experience of a lifetime--taking a student to "the Heart of the Shepherd."

Listen to David's prophetic words again and join him in this, the ultimate peak ascent of a lifetime: *"The Lord says to my Lord: 'Sit at My right hand until I make Your enemies a footstool for Your feet'"* (Psalm 110:1).

1) **Isaiah 6:1-8 -** *"In the year of King Uzziah's death I saw the Lord sitting on a throne, lofty and exalted, with the train of His robe filling the temple. Seraphim stood above Him, each having six wings: with two he covered his face, and with two he covered his feet, and with two he flew. And one called out to another and said, 'Holy, Holy, Holy, is the Lord of hosts, the whole earth is full of His glory.' And the foundations of the thresholds trembled at the voice of him who called out, while the temple was filling with smoke. Then I said, 'Woe is me, for I am ruined! Because I am a man of unclean lips, and I live among a people of unclean lips; for my eyes have seen the King, the Lord of hosts.' Then one of the seraphim flew to me with a burning coal in his hand, which he had taken from the altar with tongs. He touched my mouth with it and said, 'Behold, this has touched your lips; and your iniquity is taken away and your sin is forgiven.' Then I heard the voice of the Lord, saying, 'Whom shall I send, and who will go for Us?' Then I said, 'Here am I. Send me!'"*

   "Show and Tell" is one of the first games of kindergarten. "Show and Tell" when it comes to showing someone God and telling him or her how to experience God is certainly the greatest game of life. Why does seeing the Lord *demand* that you rise to the call to spend a lifetime taking others on the journey?

   _____

   _____

2) **2 Corinthians 12:1-4 -** *"Boasting is necessary, though it is not profitable; but I will go on to visions and revelations of the Lord. I know a man in Christ who fourteen years ago—whether in the body I do not know, or out of the body I do not know, God knows—such a man was caught up to the third heaven. And I know how such a man—whether in the body or apart from the body I do not know, God knows— was caught up into Paradise and heard inexpressible words, which a man is not permitted to speak."*

   Paul referred to his heavenly vision as the "surpassing greatness of the revelations" (v.7). Then, in response to the journey of amazement, he sacrificed himself again and again to take the message of liberation to the world. Does Paul's heroic, sacrificial calling inspire you to join him in the Great Commission? Why or why not?

   _____

   _____

3) **Revelation 4:1** - *"After these things I looked, and behold, a door standing open in heaven, and the first voice which I had heard, like the sound of a trumpet speaking with me, said, 'Come up here, and I will show you what must take place after these things.'"*

Revelation 5:11-12 - *"Then I looked, and I heard the voice of many angels around the throne and the living creatures and the elders; and the number of them was myriads of myriads, and thousands of thousands, saying with a loud voice, 'Worthy is the Lamb that was slain to receive power and riches and wisdom and might and honor and glory and blessing.'"*

Describe what John is seeing in his visual ascent.

_____

_____

How do you describe your most-memorable and -inspiring personal glimpse of Jesus' glory?

_____

_____

Are you willing to unleash yourself and guide others to that place of splendor and majesty? Why or why not?

_____

_____

4) **Exodus 34:29** - *"It came about when Moses was coming down from Mount Sinai (and the two tablets of the testimony were in Moses' hand as he was coming down from the mountain), that Moses did not know that the skin of his face shone because of his speaking with Him."*

Certainly, the experiences of David, Paul, John, Isaiah, and Moses were unique to their time and their role in presenting God's holy Word. But just as certainly, a man or woman who has a relationship with Jesus has to see Him in his or her own unique way. How does your face "shine" from seeing the Lord, and how does God want to use that shining light of your countenance to take the lost and the novice to "the holy mountain" of discipleship?

_____

_____

5) **2 Timothy 4:1-2** - *"I solemnly charge you in the presence of God and of Christ Jesus, who is to judge the living and the dead, and by His appearing and His kingdom: preach the word; be ready in season and out of season; reprove, rebuke, exhort, with great patience and instruction."*

What has today's study done to change your perspective on your calling to the Great Commission to "go and make disciples"?

_____

_____

THE SHEPHERD'S CALL

6) **John 13:15** - *"For I gave you an example that you also should do as I did to you."*

From today's scripture, how does **THE** Shepherd inspire **you** to shepherd **your** flock?

_____

_____

MINUTE OF MEDITATION

"The Lord says to my Lord: 'Sit at My right hand until I make Your enemies a footstool for Your feet'" (Psalm 110:1).

PRAYER

Adoration, **C**onfession, **T**hanksgiving, **S**upplication

Delight

"Great are the works of the Lord; they are studied by all who delight in them"
(Psalm 111:2).

Psalm 111

Listen to the amazing words used in this picturesque psalm: "all," "great," "splendid," "majestic," "wonders," "gracious," "compassionate," "fear," "power," "truth," "justice," "sure," "uprightness," "redemption," "covenant," "holy," "awesome," "wisdom," "praise," "forever" ... "DELIGHT!"

Key words in biblical study are words that are central and strategic to understanding the passage. Exclamatory words are generally adjectives that express a sudden cry of emotion, as in crying out or shouting out or expressing incredible joy or exhilaration.

Psalm 111 is filled with so many wondrous keywords of exclamation that jump from the lines of the song like fireworks colorfully and festively exploding into the sky on a star-studded Fourth of July night!

What makes the psalmist's words and meditations so remarkably different from ours today?

- Is it the psalmist's view of God?
- Is it his focus on God?
- Is it his consistent walk with God?
- Is it his intimacy with God?
- Is it all the above?

Welcome to the world of "delight." If you could slip your heart into a personality stocking that shaped the attitude of your heart and how you viewed every thought that came before your mind, what kind of stocking would you choose? Gloom? Sorrow? Anger? Criticism?

If, on the other hand, you chose to put your heart into a stocking called "delight," you'd begin to see God the way the psalmist does in this beloved psalm. A heart that delights in God is filled with joy, pleasure, glee, gusto, and exhilaration. To delight in God is to magnify all His great qualities and to implicitly trust Him with those qualities you don't understand.

To delight in God is to read Psalm 111 in the manner for which it is written. Underline the keywords of exclamation as you read.

"Praise the Lord! I will give thanks to the Lord with all my heart, in the company of the upright and in the assembly. Great are the works of the Lord; they are studied by all who delight in them. Splendid and majestic is His work, and His righteousness endures forever. He has made His wonders to be remembered; the Lord is gracious and compassionate. He has given food to those who fear Him; He will remember His covenant forever. He has made known to His people the power of His works, in giving them the heritage of the nations. The works of His hands are truth and justice; all His precepts are sure. They are upheld forever and ever; they are performed in truth and uprightness. He has sent redemption to His people; He has ordained His covenant forever; holy and awesome is His name. The fear of the Lord is the beginning of wisdom; a good understanding have all those who do His commandments; His praise endures forever" (Psalm 111).

1) **Psalm 119:16** - *"I shall delight in Your statutes; I shall not forget Your word."*

   What does it mean to you to delight in God's Word?

   _____

   _____

2) **Psalm 37:4** - *"Delight yourself in the Lord; and He will give you the desires of your heart."*

   How should the mindset of delight align you with God's will for your life?

   _____

   _____

3) **Job 22:23-26** - *"If you return to the Almighty, you will be restored; if you remove unrighteousness far from your tent, and place your gold in the dust, and the gold of Ophir among the stones of the brooks, then the Almighty will be your gold and choice silver to you. For then you will delight in the Almighty and lift up your face to God."*

   Matthew 6:24 - *"No one can serve two masters; for either he will hate the one and love the other, or he will be devoted to one and despise the other. You cannot serve God and wealth."*

   It's human nature to tend toward an attitude of entitlement. People who do well, people who are successful, and people who are blessed with talent, money, or notoriety often grow proud instead of thankful and take credit rather than give glory to God. How has the spirit of entitlement affected you?

   _____

   _____

   How do entitlement and pride rob you of your delight? How does pride dull your view of God and His astounding goodness?

   _____

   _____

4) **Psalm 119:14-15** - *"I have rejoiced in the way of Your testimonies, as much as in all riches. I will meditate on Your precepts and regard Your ways."*

   How might you develop a heart that truly and fully delights itself in God?

   _____

   _____

5) **1 Peter 1:8** - *"And though you have not seen Him, you love Him, and though you do not see Him now, but believe in Him, you greatly rejoice with joy inexpressible and full of glory."*

How can you make sure you leave an impression of "pure delight" on those you disciple and mentor?

_____

_____

THE SHEPHERD'S CALL

6) **John 13:15** - *"For I gave you an example that you also should do as I did to you."*

From today's scripture, how does **THE** Shepherd inspire **you** to shepherd **your** flock?

_____

_____

MINUTE OF MEDITATION
"Great are the works of the Lord; they are studied by all who delight in them"
(Psalm 111:2).

PRAYER
Adoration, **C**onfession, **T**hanksgiving, **S**upplication

Legacy

"Praise the Lord! How blessed is the man who fears the Lord, who greatly delights in His commandments" (Psalm 112:1).

Psalm 112

Immerse yourself in this insightful psalm, and discover the DNA of a man or woman of God and the legacy that accompanies the quest.

The person who *fears* the Lord: *"How blessed is the man who fears the Lord"* (Psalm 112:1).

The person who *delights* in God's commandments: *"Who greatly delights in His commandments"* (Psalm 112:1).

The *upright* person: *"The generation of the upright will be blessed"* (Psalm 112:2).

The *gracious* person: *"He is gracious and compassionate and righteous"* (Psalm 112:4).

The *compassionate* person: *"He is gracious and compassionate and righteous"* (Psalm 112:4).

The *righteous* person: *"He is gracious and compassionate and righteous"* (Psalm 112:4).

The *steadfast* person: *"His heart is steadfast"* (Psalm 112:7a).

The *trusting* person: *"Trusting in the Lord"* (Psalm 112:7b).

The *fearless* person: *"His heart is upheld, he will not fear"* (Psalm 112:8).

The *generous* person: *"He has given freely to the poor"* (Psalm 112:9).

Uncover, underline, and meditate on each descriptive term as you deliberate and dwell on this short but power-packed passage.

Like a giant, century-and-a-half-old Ozark Mountain bur oak tree with a trunk as wide as a Volkswagen bug, as tall as a cell tower, and with mighty branches extending as steadfastly as a tempered-steel railway carrying thousands of life-producing acorns for generations yet to come, a man or woman of God is rewarded with *legacy*, the crown jewel of God's richest blessings.

The requirements of a godly man or woman are far more rigorous than a marathon run through the mountains of southwest Missouri. I've embarked upon both endeavors, and the heavenward calling of the psalm is infinitely more demanding and equally more rewarding.

Waking up every morning with a mind set on running the race laid out for us in this psalm is the greatest race of all!

Look at the rewards offered along the way: blessed (v.1), almighty heritage (v.2), enduring righteousness (v.3), light arising in the darkness (v.4), life goes well (v.5), finish well (v.5), unshakeable (v.6), legacy (v.6), no fear (v.7), enduring righteousness (v.9), and honored (v.9).

Our mission is clear, our calling is high, and our destination is glorious. *"Let us run with endurance the race that is set before us"* (Hebrews 12:1b).

1) **1 Timothy 6:11 -** *"But flee from these things, you man of God, and pursue righteousness, godliness, faith, love, perseverance and gentleness."*

   How do you describe your personal calling to live as a man of God or a woman of God?

   _____

   _____

2) **Deuteronomy 33:1 -** *"Now this is the blessing with which Moses the man of God blessed the sons of Israel before his death."*

   How does the legacy of Ruth, Deborah, Moses, Daniel, Joseph, David, Mary, and other men and women of God inspire your heart?

   _____

   _____

3) **Psalm 78:4 -** *"We will not conceal them from their children, but tell to the generation to come the praises of the Lord, and His strength and His wondrous works that He has done."*

   Describe the legacy you desire after your days on earth are over.

   _____

   _____

4) **2 Timothy 2:22 -** *"Now flee from youthful lusts and pursue righteousness, faith, love and peace, with those who call on the Lord from a pure heart."*

   Describe the legacy of a life that is dedicated to disciple-making.

   _____

   _____

5) **Matthew 6:20-21** - *"But store up for yourselves treasures in heaven, where neither moth nor rust destroys, and where thieves do not break in or steal; for where your treasure is, there your heart will be also."*

1 Corinthians 3:11-15 - *"For no man can lay a foundation other than the one which is laid, which is Jesus Christ. Now if any man builds on the foundation with gold, silver, precious stones, wood, hay, straw, each man's work will become evident; for the day will show it because it is to be revealed with fire, and the fire itself will test the quality of each man's work. If any man's work which he has built on it remains, he will receive a reward. If any man's work is burned up, he will suffer loss; but he himself will be saved, yet so as through fire."*

Describe a heavenly legacy.

_____

_____

THE SHEPHERD'S CALL

6) **John 13:15** - *"For I gave you an example that you also should do as I did to you."*

From today's scripture, how does **THE** Shepherd inspire **you** to shepherd **your** flock?

_____

_____

MINUTE OF MEDITATION
"But flee from these things, you man of God, and pursue righteousness, godliness, faith, love, perseverance and gentleness" (1 Timothy 6:11).

PRAYER
Adoration, **C**onfession, **T**hanksgiving, **S**upplication

The Humility of the Lamb

"He raises the poor from the dust and lifts the needy from the ash heap, to make them sit with princes, with the princes of His people" (Psalm 113:7-8).

Psalm 113

The wealthiest man who ever lived was Saint Francis of Assisi, because when he gave away *everything*, all the world was his. One of the most-quoted and -admired men who ever lived, Francis said, "God could not have chosen anyone less qualified, or more of a sinner, than myself. And so, for this wonderful work He intends to perform through us, He selected me--for God always chooses the weak and the absurd, and those who count for nothing."

Francis is remembered for the time he stood in a town square and asked all his Franciscan brothers to name all his faults publicly, because he had heard too many good things being said about himself.

One of his most-noteworthy quotes reveals the depths of his meek and lowly heart as he said, "O divine master, grant me that I may not so much seek to be consoled as to console; to be understood as to understand; to be loved as to love; for it is in giving that we receive; it is in pardoning that we are pardoned; it is in dying that we are born to eternal life."

Admiring humble Christ-followers brings out true humility in the one who admires. When Head Coach Doug Pederson of the Philadelphia Eagles was first interviewed after his team won the Super Bowl, he immediately ducked the credit and proclaimed to tens of millions in the exuberant TV audience, "First of all, I want to give the glory to my Lord and Savior, Jesus Christ."

Jesus' brother James seemed to have a picture window into the heart of God when he said, *"God is opposed to the proud, but gives grace to the humble"* (James 4:6b).

1) **Psalm 113:1-3** - *"Praise the Lord! Praise, O servants of the Lord, praise the name of the Lord. Blessed be the name of the Lord from this time forth and forever. From the rising of the sun to its setting the name of the Lord is to be praised."*

   As we grow in our understanding of the greatness, the might, the sovereignty, and the majesty of God, we begin to understand what it means to walk in humility. Why is that? How can we maintain that perspective throughout a busy day?

   _____
   _____

2) **Psalm 113:4-6** - *"The Lord is high above all nations; His glory is above the heavens. Who is like the Lord our God, who is enthroned on high, who humbles Himself to behold the things that are in heaven and in the earth?"*

   Psalm 8:4 - *"What is man that You take thought of him, and the son of man that You care for him?"*

   It is mind-blowing that the God of the universe would humble Himself to care deeply for His people on the tiny speck of dust in the cosmos on which we live! How does His humility affect yours?
   _____
   _____

   Why does the humble lamb go deeper in his love, praise, and fear of his Shepherd?
   _____
   _____

3) **Proverbs 18:12** - *"Before destruction the heart of man is haughty, but humility goes before honor."*

   There are five seasons in the year: winter, spring, summer, pride, fall. When do you struggle the most with false humility and pride?
   _____
   _____

4) **Colossians 3:12** - *"So, as those who have been chosen of God, holy and beloved, put on a heart of compassion, kindness, humility, gentleness and patience."*

   What does it mean for a true seeker of God's heart to "put on" humility?
   _____
   _____

   What makes humble people so attractive?
   _____
   _____

5) **1 Peter 5:6** - *"Therefore humble yourselves under the mighty hand of God, that He may exalt you at the proper time."*

   Why is it in God's nature to exalt the humble heart?
   _____
   _____

THE SHEPHERD'S CALL

6) **John 13:15** - *"For I gave you an example that you also should do as I did to you."*

From today's scripture, how does **THE** Shepherd inspire **you** to shepherd **your** flock?

_____

_____

MINUTE OF MEDITATION
"Before destruction the heart of man is haughty, but humility goes before honor" (Proverbs 18:12).

PRAYER
Adoration, Confession, Thanksgiving, Supplication

Deliverance

"When Israel went forth from Egypt, the house of Jacob from a people of strange language, Judah became His sanctuary, Israel, His dominion. The sea looked and fled; the Jordan turned back. The mountains skipped like rams, the hills, like lambs" (Psalm 114:1-4).

Psalm 114

Depression is a deep, thick, stormy, gray cloud that travels ominously over the emotional sky of a person's heart 24 hours a day, seven days a week. The cloud seems permanent and immoveable. It's reinforced with layers of sadness, worry, fear, and personal defeat.

I've been under the cloud twice--once as a young college football coach, and once as an older ministry leader. I cried during those dark days until it felt as if my tear ducts became barren and ran out of tears to shed.

With very few exceptions through decades of counseling and coaching others through the difficult journey, the good news is twofold. First, *God delivers.* Second, the cloud is not static. It's a moving target. Best of all, however, is the scriptural truth that looking back on the journey, God gives you 20/20 vision to see His constructive, purposeful hand every step of the way.

Deliverance from addictions of every class and genre is God's specialty. As He liberated His chosen people from bondage in Egypt, parting the Red Sea, providing food for their journey, giving the Ten Commandments and His presence in the tabernacle to guide their way, so God *will* deliver every *willing* heart from any form of enslavement. *"What ails you, O sea, that you flee? O Jordan, that you turn back? O mountains, that you skip like rams? O hills, like lambs? Tremble, O earth, before the Lord, before the God of Jacob, Who turned the rock into a pool of water, the flint into a fountain of water"* (Psalm 114:5-8).

1) **Galatians 5:1** - *"It was for freedom that Christ set us free; therefore keep standing firm and do not be subject again to a yoke of slavery."* How did Jesus set us free once and for all time? How can He keep us free on a daily basis?

   _____

   _____

2) **Psalm 34:17** - *"The righteous cry, and the Lord hears and delivers them out of all their troubles."*

   Psalm 50:15 - *"Call upon Me in the day of trouble; I shall rescue you, and you will honor Me."*

   The Greek word for *deliverance* is *soteria,* which translates to "salvation, welfare, prosperity, preservation, and safety." Describe how God delivers you from your worst times of emotional bondage, sin, or addiction.

   _____

   _____

How can His liberating Spirit aid in your deliverance?

_____

_____

3) **James 5:16** - *"Therefore, confess your sins to one another, and pray for one another so that you may be healed. The effective prayer of a righteous man can accomplish much."*

How can walking and praying with a caring Christian brother or sister in an accountability relationship make deliverance come more readily and succeed in the long term?

_____

_____

4) **Colossians 1:13** - *"For He rescued us from the domain of darkness, and transferred us to the kingdom of His beloved Son."*
How does deliverance produce deep gratitude and praise? Describe the depth of your heart's gratitude to the One who *has* delivered and *will* deliver you.

_____

_____

5) **Romans 7:18-20, 24-25a** - *"For I know that nothing good dwells in me, that is, in my flesh; for the willing is present in me, but the doing of the good is not. For the good that I want, I do not do, but I practice the very evil that I do not want. But if I am doing the very thing I do not want, I am no longer the one doing it, but sin which dwells in me. ... Wretched man that I am! Who will set me free from the body of this death? Thanks be to God through Jesus Christ our Lord!"*

Romans 8:1 - *"Therefore there is now no condemnation for those who are in Christ Jesus."*

How do you relate to Paul's famous words in this Romans 7-8 discourse?

_____

_____

THE SHEPHERD'S CALL
6) **John 13:15** - *"For I gave you an example that you also should do as I did to you."*

From today's scripture, how does **THE** Shepherd inspire **you** to shepherd **your** flock?

_____

_____

MINUTE OF MEDITATION

"The righteous cry, and the Lord hears and delivers them out of all their troubles" (Psalm 34:17).

PRAYER

Adoration, Confession, Thanksgiving, Supplication

Idols

"Not to us, O Lord, not to us, but to Your name give glory because of Your lovingkindness, because of Your truth" (Psalm 115:1).

Psalm 115

Jesus, "the Great Shepherd of the sheep," delivers well the warning of the pitfalls for every footstep taken through the counterfeit doorway by the one who would bring a lamb into destruction: *"Truly, truly, I say to you, he who does not enter by the door into the fold of the sheep, but climbs up some other way, he is a thief and a robber"* (John 10:1).

Some idols are large and audacious. Some are small and subtle. Some idols destroy a Christ-follower quickly; most destroy slowly. Some idols are obvious; most are elusive.

The successful fisherman and the successful counterfeit-money-producer have one thing in common with the enemy of our soul. They are both experts in fake reproduction. The sharp, barbed treble hooks on the fishing lure sink deep into the fishes' mouths when the replica is foolishly taken, and the fish finds itself in the frying pan, scorched by the heat of the fire.

So it is with Satan and his skillful use of idols. Hear the words of the psalmist: *"Their idols are silver and gold, the work of man's hands. They have mouths, but they cannot speak; they have eyes, but they cannot see; they have ears, but they cannot hear; they have noses, but they cannot smell; they have hands, but they cannot feel; they have feet, but they cannot walk; they cannot make a sound with their throat. Those who make them will become like them, everyone who trusts in them"* (Psalm 115:4-8).

Lust can look a lot like love. Many a young fool has fallen by getting high on alcohol, pot, nicotine, porn, and prescription drugs that can feel a lot like getting high on Jesus. Many are the stimulants to which dopamine responds and flows through the brain. All are addictive and have treble hooks that take the fish to the frying pan.

"Just try it once ..."
"A little sip won't hurt you ..."
"As long as you don't go all the way ..."
"This will make it safe ..."
"As long as it's love, it's okay ..."
"It's not really smoke, it's just vape ..."
"There's just a few bad words, but you hardly even notice them ..."

Sound familiar? Satan has many mouths. He whispers through the ears of the naive with crafty vigilance. *"Whose end is destruction, whose god is their appetite, and whose glory is in their shame, who set their minds on earthly things"* (Philippians 3:19).

1) **Psalm 115:9-13** - *"O Israel, trust in the Lord; He is their help and their shield. O house of Aaron, trust in the Lord; He is their help and their shield. You who fear the Lord, trust in the Lord; He is their help and their shield. The Lord has been mindful of us; He will bless us; He will bless the house of Israel; He will bless the house of Aaron. He will bless those who fear the Lord, the small together with the great."*

   Name three ways the Lord shields us, warns us, and protects us from idols and dangerous temptations.

   _____

   _____

2) **John 14:16** - *"I will ask the Father, and He will give you another Helper, that He may be with you forever."*

   John 16:1 - *"These things I have spoken to you so that you may be kept from stumbling."*

   What is the role of the Holy Spirit in the life of a Christ-follower?

   _____

   _____

3) **Ephesians 4:30** - *"Do not grieve the Holy Spirit of God, by whom you were sealed for the day of redemption."*

   1 Thessalonians 5:15 - *"See that no one repays another with evil for evil, but always seek after that which is good for one another and for all people."*

   How do you "grieve" the Spirit?

   _____

   _____

   How do you quench the Spirit?

   _____

   _____

   What is the result of either?

   _____

   _____

4) **Proverbs 29:23** - *"A man's pride will bring him low, but a humble spirit will obtain honor."*

   Why is pride a deceitful idol?

   _____

   _____

5) **Psalm 115:18** - *"But as for us, we will bless the Lord from this time forth and forever. Praise the Lord!"*

How does praise eradicate pride?

_____

_____

THE SHEPHERD'S CALL

6) **John 13:15** - *"For I gave you an example that you also should do as I did to you."*

From today's scripture, how does **THE** Shepherd inspire **you** to shepherd **your** flock?

_____

_____

MINUTE OF MEDITATION
"I will ask the Father, and He will give you another Helper, that He may be with you forever" (John 14:16).

PRAYER
Adoration, **C**onfession, **T**hanksgiving, **S**upplication

The Prayer of the Lamb

"I love the Lord, because He hears my voice and my supplications"
(Psalm 116:1).

Psalm 116

Creating the cosmos in six days? Easy work for an *all*-powerful God who exists supernaturally outside of time. If God is indeed omnipotent, He could have done it in 6 nanoseconds! But keeping up with 7 billion sheep on His chosen planet ... now, that's an impressive job!

One of Jesus' most-beloved teachings that exposes God's tenderness toward the tiny, prayerful outcry of one of His most-remotely secluded lambs is the one about the lost lamb. Listen to Jesus' words as if you're hearing them for the first time:

"What man among you, if he has a hundred sheep and has lost one of them, does not leave the ninety-nine in the open pasture and go after the one which is lost until he finds it? When he has found it, he lays it on his shoulders, rejoicing. And when he comes home, he calls together his friends and his neighbors, saying to them, 'Rejoice with me, for I have found my sheep which was lost!' I tell you that in the same way, there will be more joy in heaven over one sinner who repents than over ninety-nine righteous persons who need no repentance" (Luke 15:4-7).

An interviewer once asked the deeply devoted Mother Teresa, "What do you say when you pray?"

She answered, "Nothing." Then, surprisingly, she continued to say, "I listen."

The interviewer pressed in, "What does God say when you pray?"

She responded yet again, "Nothing. He listens."

God listens. As He towers and infiltrates above, beyond, throughout, and within, the Almighty God listens. After 70 years of praying thousands of prayers, I could tell you countless stories I've personally experienced where God so obviously heard my prayers and clearly, consistently, and deliberately answered them. Prayers of restoration, prayers of vision, prayers of relationship repair, prayers of healing, prayers of the needs of others; the list is endless. But the greatest prayer gift of all is that God listens.

"This is the confidence which we have before Him, that, if we ask anything according to His will, He hears us. And if we know that He hears us in whatever we ask, we know that we have the requests which we have asked from Him" (1 John 5:14-15).

1) **Psalm 116:2** - *"Because He has inclined His ear to me, therefore I shall call upon Him as long as I live."*

   Think for a second, how many texts and phone calls do you make a day? _____

   How many "God calls" do you make a day? _____

   What's it like for you to know that He always picks up your call?

   _____

   _____

2) **Psalm 116:3-5** - *"The cords of death encompassed me and the terrors of Sheol came upon me; I found distress and sorrow. Then I called upon the name of the Lord: 'O Lord, I beseech You, save my life!' Gracious is the Lord, and righteous; yes, our God is compassionate."*

   Recall the time in your life when you most-closely related to the psalmist in this passage. How did God pull you through it?

   _____

   _____

3) **Matthew 7:7-8** - *"Ask, and it will be given to you; seek, and you will find; knock, and it will be opened to you. For everyone who asks receives, and he who seeks finds, and to him who knocks it will be opened."*

   It has been aptly said that the worst thing God could do for us is to give us what we want when our desires are outside His perfect will for our lives. How can God say, "Not yet," "Not now," or "No" to our prayers and still be 100 percent reliable?

   _____

   _____

4) **Psalm 27:8** - *"When You said, 'Seek My face,' my heart said to You, 'Your face, O Lord, I shall seek.'"*

   2 Chronicles 6:21 - *"Listen to the supplications of Your servant and of Your people Israel when they pray toward this place; hear from Your dwelling place, from heaven; hear and forgive."*

   When we pray, why is it far better to seek His face than to seek His hands?

   _____

   _____

5) **2 Chronicles 7:14** - *"And My people who are called by My name humble themselves and pray and seek My face and turn from their wicked ways, then I will hear from heaven, will forgive their sin and will heal their land."*

Humble yourself. Pray. Seek His face. Turn from your wicked ways. *Then* God hears, forgives, and heals. What's God asking you to do as you read this passage?

_____

_____

6) **Luke 6:12** - *"It was at this time that He went off to the mountain to pray, and He spent the whole night in prayer to God."*

If even Jesus needed time alone with His Father, what does that say about *your* need?

_____

_____

THE SHEPHERD'S CALL

7) **John 13:15** - *"For I gave you an example that you also should do as I did to you."*

From today's scripture, how does **THE** Shepherd inspire **you** to shepherd **your** flock?

_____

_____

MINUTE OF MEDITATION

"Because He has inclined His ear to me, therefore I shall call upon Him as long as I live" (Psalm 116:2).

PRAYER

Adoration, **C**onfession, **T**hanksgiving, **S**upplication

God Our Shelter

"It is better to take refuge in the Lord than to trust in princes" (Psalm 118:9).

"While we look not at the things which are seen, but at the things which are not seen; for the things which are seen are temporal, but the things which are not seen are eternal" (2 Corinthians 4:18).

Psalm 118

To a baby girl, it's her mother's arms.
To a mom, it's being surrounded by a loving family.
To a musician, it's a quiet, secluded room to write in.
To an artist, it's a remote mountain waterfall.
To a lost lamb, it's in the safekeeping of his shepherd.
To King David in his boyhood, it was the big, starry sky above. As a young man, it was an unknown, rocky cave hiding him safely from an angry King Saul. In his latter years, it was his walled city.
Refuge ... it's our safe place; it's a Christian's place of security, provision, and shelter.
Everybody needs a refuge. Without one, life can be a frightening experience.

In an ever deepening, intimate, abiding relationship with Jesus, a Christ-follower who *stays* in fellowship with "the Great Shepherd of the Sheep" is never without a refuge. Never!

"God is our refuge and strength, a very present help in trouble. Therefore we will not fear, though the earth should change and though the mountains slip into the heart of the sea; though its waters roar and foam, though the mountains quake at its swelling pride" (Psalm 46:1-3).

Forgive me for dropping names, but the point of the story is worth the risk. I was fortunate to have a couple of warm chats with America's 43rd president, George W. Bush. That man is one of the most-sincere, kind-hearted, and humble individuals on an interpersonal level I've ever met.

He often retreated at Camp David with his wife and closest advisors during his eight-year term in the White House. He also loved to join his mom and dad on occasion at their getaway in Kennebunkport, Maine, on the Atlantic coast. And he certainly loved a few days away from the Oval Office on getaways to his ranch in Crawford, Texas.

But, as the most-powerful man in the world, his refuge--his only truly safe and 100 percent-trusted shelter--was his prayer time, his Bible time, and his morning devotionals in the Oswald Chambers book *My Utmost for His Highest*, which he read almost every morning.

With the most-powerful army, air force, marines, navy, and coast guard in the world readily deployed with a mere phone call, that man was painfully aware that there *is* no true refuge except for the place Isaiah described so vividly:

"For You have been a defense for the helpless, a defense for the needy in his distress, a refuge from the storm, a shade from the heat; for the breath of the ruthless is like a rain storm against a wall" (Isaiah 25:4).

1) **Luke 9:58** - *"The foxes have holes and the birds of the air have nests, but the Son of Man has nowhere to lay His head."*

   Luke 6:12 - *"It was at this time that He went off to the mountain to pray, and He spent the whole night in prayer to God."*

   September 11, 2001 was all the evidence our 43rd president needed. Jesus was well aware of that which "Bush 43" found to be true: As Creator of the cosmos and beyond, Jesus had no safe place on this earth with the exception of the times He spent alone, fellowshipping with His Father. How does this idea speak to you?

   _____

   _____

2) **Ecclesiastes 2:1-4, 10-11** - *"I said to myself, 'Come now, I will test you with pleasure. So enjoy yourself.' And behold, it too was futility. I said of laughter, 'It is madness,' and of pleasure, 'What does it accomplish?' I explored with my mind how to stimulate my body with wine while my mind was guiding me wisely, and how to take hold of folly, until I could see what good there is for the sons of men to do under heaven the few years of their lives. I enlarged my works: I built houses for myself, I planted vineyards for myself. ... All that my eyes desired I did not refuse them. I did not withhold my heart from any pleasure, for my heart was pleased because of all my labor and this was my reward for all my labor. Thus I considered all my activities which my hands had done and the labor which I had exerted, and behold all was vanity and striving after wind and there was no profit under the sun."*

   Where do you tend to run when you need a refuge? Why?

   _____

   _____

   What are you learning from the emptiness of false refuges?

   _____

   _____

3) **Philippians 1:12-14** - *"Now I want you to know, brethren, that my circumstances have turned out for the greater progress of the gospel, so that my imprisonment in the cause of Christ has become well known throughout the whole praetorian guard and to everyone else, and that most of the brethren, trusting in the Lord because of my imprisonment, have far more courage to speak the word of God without fear."*

Philippians 3:8-10 - *"More than that, I count all things to be loss in view of the surpassing value of knowing Christ Jesus my Lord, for whom I have suffered the loss of all things, and count them but rubbish so that I may gain Christ, and may be found in Him, not having a righteousness of my own derived from the Law, but that which is through faith in Christ, the righteousness which comes from God on the basis of faith, that I may know Him and the power of His resurrection and the fellowship of His sufferings, being conformed to His death."*

What did Paul learn about his true refuge, and what does Paul's life teach you?

_____

_____

4) **Psalm 91:2** - *"I will say to the Lord, 'My refuge and my fortress, my God, in whom I trust!'"*

Proverbs 14:26 - *"In the fear of the Lord there is strong confidence, and his children will have refuge."*

How can you increase the strength and security of your true refuge? How do you intend to accomplish your aim?

_____

_____

5) **Ephesians 3:14-19** - *"For this reason I bow my knees before the Father, from whom every family in heaven and on earth derives its name, that He would grant you, according to the riches of His glory, to be strengthened with power through His Spirit in the inner man, so that Christ may dwell in your hearts through faith; and that you, being rooted and grounded in love, may be able to comprehend with all the saints what is the breadth and length and height and depth, and to know the love of Christ which surpasses knowledge, that you may be filled up to all the fullness of God."*

How does this doxology help you better understand your only reliable refuge?

_____

_____

THE SHEPHERD'S CALL

6) **John 13:15** - *"For I gave you an example that you also should do as I did to you."*

From today's scripture, how does **THE** Shepherd inspire **you** to shepherd **your** flock?

_____

_____

MINUTE OF MEDITATION

"For You have been a defense for the helpless, a defense for the needy in his distress, a refuge from the storm, a shade from the heat; for the breath of the ruthless is like a rain storm against a wall" (Isaiah 25:4).

PRAYER

Adoration, Confession, Thanksgiving, Supplication

The Word of the Shepherd

"Your word is a lamp to my feet and a light to my path" (Psalm 119:105).

Psalm 119

Out on the mountainside, the shepherd communicates clearly with his flock through the skillful use of his rod, his staff, his voice, and in many cases his sheepdog. As a well-trained sheepdog understands and respects the voice of his master, so you and I have a direct line to the voice of God. No place in Scripture describes that great truth more thoroughly than Psalm 119.

A depressed and bewildered college student who worked on our camp staff sought me out for counsel one summer day many years ago. I had known her for several years and was aware that her condition was chronic and had crippled her emotional health for some years. Our counseling session was surprisingly short, but I assumed it would be only the beginning of the solution to her deep psychological issues. After we prayed, I asked her to go memorize Psalm 119:1-11.

To my great surprise, three days later she came back and said, "It worked! I did it. God took my depression away as I was memorizing and meditating on those verses." As long as I knew her after that startling day, she never fell back into depression again.

"For the word of God is living and active and sharper than any two-edged sword, and piercing as far as the division of soul and spirit, of both joints and marrow, and able to judge the thoughts and intentions of the heart" (Hebrews 4:12).

1) **Psalm 119:1-4** - *"How blessed are those whose way is blameless, who walk in the law of the Lord. How blessed are those who observe His testimonies, who seek Him with all their heart. They also do no unrighteousness; they walk in His ways. You have ordained Your precepts, that we should keep them diligently."*

   What does "diligently" mean in this passage?

   _____
   _____

   What does the phrase "all their heart" mean?

   _____
   _____

   What does it mean to "walk in the law of the Lord?"

   _____
   _____

2) **Psalm 119:9-11** - *"How can a young man keep his way pure? By keeping it according to Your word. With all my heart I have sought You; do not let me wander from Your commandments. Your word I have treasured in my heart, that I may not sin against You."*

Why and how is it true that "treasuring" and "keeping" God's Word keeps you from sin and develops a pure heart?

_____

_____

3) **Psalm 119:14-16** - *"I have rejoiced in the way of Your testimonies, as much as in all riches. I will meditate on Your precepts and regard Your ways. I shall delight in Your statutes; I shall not forget Your word."*

In this wonderful passage, the psalmist combines an attitude of "rejoicing over and delighting in" God's Word with the practice of meditating on that which he had memorized. What makes that combination so productive?

_____

_____

4) **Psalm 119:18** - *"Open my eyes, that I may behold wonderful things from Your law."*

What a prayer before your daily reading of God's Word!

Ephesians 1:18 - *"I pray that the eyes of your heart may be enlightened, so that you will know what is the hope of His calling, what are the riches of the glory of His inheritance in the saints."*

What are "the eyes of your heart"? What are the psalmist and Paul asking you for?

_____

_____

5) **Psalm 119:24** - *"Your testimonies also are my delight; they are my counselors."*

Psalm 32:8 - *"I will instruct you and teach you in the way which you should go; I will counsel you with My eye upon you."*

Psalm 16:7 - *"I will bless the Lord who has counseled me; indeed, my mind instructs me in the night."*

A good biblical counselor coaches a client through psychological and emotional difficulties. How does meditation on Scripture actually "counsel you" and "instruct you in the night"?

_____

_____

6) **Psalm 119:28** - *"My soul weeps because of grief; strengthen me according to Your word."*

"Strengthen me," "make me understand," "remove the false way from me," "enlarge my heart," "teach me," "turn my eyes from vanity," "revive me," "comfort me in my affliction," "take away my reproach." As you review Psalm 119 and see *all* the truths the psalmist ascribes to God's Word, how does this psalm inspire *you*?

_____

_____

THE SHEPHERD'S CALL

7) **John 13:15** - *"For I gave you an example that you also should do as I did to you."*

From today's scripture, how does **THE** Shepherd inspire **you** to shepherd **your** flock?

_____

_____

MINUTE OF MEDITATION

"How can a young man keep his way pure? By keeping it according to Your word. With all my heart I have sought You; do not let me wander from Your commandments. Your word I have treasured in my heart, that I may not sin against You" (Psalm 119:9-11).

PRAYER

Adoration, **C**onfession, **T**hanksgiving, **S**upplication

The Keeper of the Flock

"He will not allow your foot to slip; He who keeps you will not slumber. Behold, He who keeps Israel will neither slumber nor sleep" (Psalm 121:3-4).

Psalm 121

Alexander III of Macedon, better known as Alexander the Great, conquered Persia under the rule of Darius III in 334 BC. During his quest to conquer and rule most of the civilized world, this son of King Philip II was loathed by many a man across Asia. Knowing his father had been assassinated and that his life also lay in jeopardy, every night when he closed his eyes he was asked, "How do you sleep at night?"

His reply was simply, "Because my guards do not sleep."

How do *you* sleep at night? When anxiety, fear, spiritual warfare, worries about tomorrow, and difficult memories of yesterday hem you in on every side ... Sominex? Lunesta? Restoria? Ambien? Desyrel? Valium? In this, one of the "psalms of ascent" that the Hebrew people would sing as they climbed the 2,510-foot Temple mount to "meet with and worship Jehovah," the psalmist cries out with great comfort, peace, praise, and joy that "God is my bodyguard." He is my keeper. My soul rests in Him.

"[He] made heaven and earth" (v.2). The God who created the cosmos and holds it together made me, and He will hold my life together! *"He will not allow your foot to slip."* The God who invented gravity, mobility, flight, motion, and all of life will hold you up when everything around you falls apart! He *"will neither sleep nor slumber."* He is your 24/7/365 bodyguard. *"The Lord is your shade on your right hand"* (v.5). He is as close as your shadow! *"The Lord will protect you from all evil"* (v.7a). He wins all battles of your spiritual warfare. *"He will keep your soul"* (v.7b). In Christ, your eternity is secure. He died on a cross to that end. *"The Lord will guard your going out and your coming in"* (v.8). God is good *all the time. All the time. All the time.*

Benjamin Franklin must have placed his anchor upon this firm foundation as he proclaimed, "I look upon death to be as necessary to our constitution as sleep. I shall rise refreshed in the morning."

1) **John 17:2** - *"Even as You gave Him authority over all flesh, that to all whom You have given Him, He may give eternal life."*

   What is "Jesus, the Keeper of the Flock," proclaiming in this verse as He prayed for His disciples in the Upper Room on the night before His crucifixion?

   _____

   _____

2) **Jude 24-25** - *"Now to Him who is able to keep you from stumbling, and to make you stand in the presence of His glory blameless with great joy, to the only God our Savior, through Jesus Christ our Lord, be glory, majesty, dominion and authority, before all time and now and forever. Amen."*

How does this beloved doxology comfort you in the midst of the trials, worries, and fears that surround you?

_____

_____

3) **Ephesians 6:12** - *"For our struggle is not against flesh and blood, but against the rulers, against the powers, against the world forces of this darkness, against the spiritual forces of wickedness in the heavenly places."*

   2 Corinthians 10:4 - *"For the weapons of our warfare are not of the flesh, but divinely powerful for the destruction of fortresses."*

   Describe in your own words how God is your keeper in the midst of spiritual warfare.

_____

_____

4) **Matthew 10:28-31** - *"Do not fear those who kill the body but are unable to kill the soul; but rather fear Him who is able to destroy both soul and body in hell. Are not two sparrows sold for a cent? And yet not one of them will fall to the ground apart from your Father. But the very hairs of your head are all numbered. So do not fear; you are more valuable than many sparrows.*

   What place does fear have in your life if you truly believe God is your keeper?

_____

_____

5) **Philippians 1:6** - *"For I am confident of this very thing, that He who began a good work in you will perfect it until the day of Christ Jesus."*

   What does this verse suggest about your plans for today?

_____

_____

THE SHEPHERD'S CALL

6) **John 13:15** - *"For I gave you an example that you also should do as I did to you."*

   From today's scripture, how does **THE** Shepherd inspire **you** to shepherd **your** flock?

_____

_____

MINUTE OF MEDITATION
"He will not allow your foot to slip; He who keeps you will not slumber. Behold, He who keeps Israel will neither slumber nor sleep" (Psalm 121:3-4).

PRAYER
Adoration, Confession, Thanksgiving, Supplication

The House of Our Shepherd

"I was glad when they said to me, let us go to the house of the Lord"
(Psalm 122:1).

Psalm 122

The Oval Office of the president of the United States, located in the West Wing of the White House, is an awe-inspiring visit for a patriotic American. The current space was built by Franklin Delano Roosevelt in 1934 and features various historic paintings, a fireplace, an impressive grandfather clock, a beautiful rug with the seal of the president, and the Resolute Desk made from the timbers of the British frigate *HMS Resolute*. This magnificent desk was presented to President Rutherford B. Hayes in 1880 by Queen Victoria. The office is respected throughout the world as the workplace of the most-powerful person in the world. A tour of the White House and a chance to walk in the footprints of dozens of U.S. presidents who have served there is an experience of a lifetime.

Imagine how the Jews felt when they had an opportunity to visit the "house of God" (*Beit HaMikdash*). The Holy Temple was located 2,500 feet above sea level atop Mount Moriah in central Jerusalem. Built with extreme attention to detail and overlaid with sheets of gold in much of its interior, this 180-by-90-by-50-feet monumental wonder was "where God lived." Hear the words of King Solomon: *"The house which I am about to build will be great, for greater is our God than all the gods. But who is able to build a house for Him, for the heavens and the highest heavens cannot contain Him? So who am I, that I should build a house for Him, except to burn incense before Him?"* (2 Chronicles 2:5-6)

But Solomon did as he was instructed and completed the Temple, which featured behind the veil the inner sanctuary, the Holy of Holies, which housed the greatest treasure: the Ark of the Covenant, with its golden cherubim with wings spread over the Mercy Seat.

Solomon praised God upon the completion of his work: *"Now therefore arise, O Lord God, to Your resting place, You and the ark of Your might; let Your priests, O Lord God, be clothed with salvation and let Your godly ones rejoice in what is good"* (2 Chronicles 6:41).

There has never been, nor will there ever be, a place in this world as revered, as adorned, as feared, and as praised as the Temple of God, the house of the Lord, the crown jewel of Israel.

1) **2 Chronicles 5:12-13** - *"And all the Levitical singers, Asaph, Heman, Jeduthun, and their sons and kinsmen, clothed in fine linen, with cymbals, harps and lyres, standing east of the altar, and with them one hundred and twenty priests blowing trumpets in unison when the trumpeters and the singers were to make themselves heard with one voice to praise and to glorify the Lord, and when they lifted up their voice accompanied by trumpets and cymbals and instruments of music, and when they praised the Lord saying, 'He indeed is good for His lovingkindness is everlasting,' then the house, the house of the Lord, was filled with a cloud."*

   When you read of the high praise the Hebrew nation offered up to God in the house of the Lord, what does that suggest about how our worship today should look?

   _____

   _____

2) **2 Chronicles 7:4-5** - *"Then the king and all the people offered sacrifice before the Lord. King Solomon offered a sacrifice of 22,000 oxen and 120,000 sheep. Thus the king and all the people dedicated the house of God."*

   Romans 12:1-2 - *"Therefore I urge you, brethren, by the mercies of God, to present your bodies a living and holy sacrifice, acceptable to God, which is your spiritual service of worship. And do not be conformed to this world, but be transformed by the renewing of your mind, so that you may prove what the will of God is, that which is good and acceptable and perfect."*

   What does it mean to offer your body as a living sacrifice?

   _____

   _____

   How do you compare the extravagant sacrifices made to God in His Temple to the idea that your life is called to be a living sacrifice?

   _____

   _____

3) **1 Corinthians 6:18-20** - *"Flee immorality. Every other sin that a man commits is outside the body, but the immoral man sins against his own body. Or do you not know that your body is a temple of the Holy Spirit who is in you, whom you have from God, and that you are not your own? For you have been bought with a price: therefore glorify God in your body."*

   What does it mean that "your body is a temple"?

   _____

   _____

In the context of the holiness, the high honor, and the extreme awe and respect due to God in the Temple of Jerusalem, what does this New Testament exhortation say about the things you allow into your mind through what you see, what you hear, what you inhale, what you eat and drink, what you touch, and what your mind dwells upon?

_____

_____

4) **Hebrews 9:11-12** - *"But when Christ appeared as a high priest of the good things to come, He entered through the greater and more perfect tabernacle, not made with hands, that is to say, not of this creation; and not through the blood of goats and calves, but through His own blood, He entered the holy place once for all, having obtained eternal redemption."*

Hebrews 10:19-22 - *"Therefore, brethren, since we have confidence to enter the holy place by the blood of Jesus, by a new and living way which He inaugurated for us through the veil, that is, His flesh, and since we have a great priest over the house of God, let us draw near with a sincere heart in full assurance of faith, having our hearts sprinkled clean from an evil conscience and our bodies washed with pure water."*

Describe the painstaking work of Jesus on the cross as it relates to your access to the house of the Lord.

_____

_____

How should you spend the rest of your life in light of this astounding, historic proclamation?

_____

_____

THE SHEPHERD'S CALL
5) **John 13:15** - *"For I gave you an example that you also should do as I did to you."*

From today's scripture, how does **THE** Shepherd inspire **you** to shepherd **your** flock?

_____

_____

MINUTE OF MEDITATION

"But when Christ appeared as a high priest of the good things to come, He entered through the greater and more perfect tabernacle, not made with hands, that is to say, not of this creation; and not through the blood of goats and calves, but through His own blood, He entered the holy place once for all, having obtained eternal redemption" (Hebrews 9:11-12).

PRAYER

Adoration, **C**onfession, **T**hanksgiving, **S**upplication

The Eyes of the Lamb

"To You I lift up my eyes, O You who are enthroned in the heavens! Behold, as the eyes of servants look to the hand of their master, as the eyes of a maid to the hand of her mistress, so our eyes look to the Lord our God, until He is gracious to us. Be gracious to us, O Lord, be gracious to us, for we are greatly filled with contempt" (Psalm 123:1-3).

Psalm 123

The complexity and capacity of the human eye are mind-boggling! The retina of your eye has 10 million cells, tiny machines unmatched by any ever built by man. Every thousandth of a second, each of those cells performs 500 nonlinear differential equations 100 times each! Talk about a calculus assignment! That's why Darwin himself said, in his renowned book *On the Origin of Species*, "To suppose that the eye, with all its inimitable contrivances for adjusting the focus to different distances, for admitting different amounts of light, and for the correction of spherical and chromatic aberration, could have been formed by natural selection, seems, I freely confess, absurd in the highest possible degree."

The eye controls the mind like a steering wheel controlling the position of a car. Our eyes are our guide. They set the course of our thinking and our activities. They also print pictures into our minds that we never forget. As they bring pictures into the mind (good or bad), the brain produces epinephrine, which prints the picture into the memory like a face carved into Mount Rushmore. That's why porn is *so* lethal. I'll bet that's why focusing on God is *so* preservative.

The whole human eye contains about 100 million cells, each with the capacity of one 10 million bytes of information per second (1.25 megabytes). The amount of care, caution, and respect a Christ-follower should give to the direction and point of focus of his eyes, in terms of the thoughts he wants to produce and the words and actions by which he lives, is monumental. That's why Jesus taught His followers, in His famous Sermon on the Mount, *"The eye is the lamp of the body; so then if your eye is clear, your whole body will be full of light. But if your eye is bad, your whole body will be full of darkness. If then the light that is in you is darkness, how great is the darkness"* (Matthew 6:22-23).

Because Jesus designed and constructed the eye "from the beginning of creation," He is no doubt the greatest authority on this profound word of caution.

1) **Colossians 3:1-2** - *"Therefore if you have been raised up with Christ, keep seeking the things above, where Christ is, seated at the right hand of God. Set your mind on the things above, not on the things that are on earth."*

   What does it mean to "set your mind"?
   _____
   _____

2) **Psalm 119:18** - *"Open my eyes, that I may behold wonderful things from Your law."*

What is the psalmist petitioning God for?

_____

_____

How does this inspire your Bible reading?

_____

_____

3) **Proverbs 4:25** - *"Let your eyes look directly ahead and let your gaze be fixed straight in front of you."*

Psalm 119:37 - *"Turn away my eyes from looking at vanity, and revive me in Your ways."*

How do these passages speak to you?

_____

_____

4) **Ephesians 1:18** - *"I pray that the eyes of your heart may be enlightened, so that you will know what is the hope of His calling, what are the riches of the glory of His inheritance in the saints."*

Philippians 4:8 - *"Finally, brethren, whatever is true, whatever is honorable, whatever is right, whatever is pure, whatever is lovely, whatever is of good repute, if there is any excellence and if anything worthy of praise, dwell on these things."*

What are "the eyes of your heart"?

_____

_____

According to Philippians 4:8, where should "the eyes of your heart" be focused?

_____

_____

5) **1 John 2:16** - *"For all that is in the world, the lust of the flesh and the lust of the eyes and the boastful pride of life, is not from the Father, but is from the world."*

What is this verse communicating to you?

_____

_____

6) **Job 31:1** - *"I have made a covenant with my eyes; how then could I gaze at a virgin?"*

What would it mean in your daily life if you made such a covenant with your eyes?

_____

_____

THE SHEPHERD'S CALL

7) **John 13:15** - *"For I gave you an example that you also should do as I did to you."*

From today's scripture, how does **THE** Shepherd inspire **you** to shepherd **your** flock?

_____

_____

MINUTE OF MEDITATION
"I pray that the eyes of your heart may be enlightened, so that you will know what is the hope of His calling, what are the riches of the glory of His inheritance in the saints" (Ephesians 1:18).

PRAYER
Adoration, **C**onfession, **T**hanksgiving, **S**upplication

Homebuilding

"Unless the Lord builds the house, they labor in vain who build it"
(Psalm 127:1a).

Psalm 127

Forty-six wonderful, crazy, wild, rambunctious years ago, I placed a wedding band on the left hand of the one Debbie-Jo Downs of Scottsdale, Arizona. We were as naïve as it gets about what it takes to build a family. All I knew was that I was madly in love with her and wanted to spend every second of every day of the rest of my life with her. (Crazy thing is, after almost half a century together, I still feel the same way about that girl of mine!)

Next thing we knew, we had four kids to raise, bills to pay, hungry little mouths to feed, diapers to change, laundry to fold, spills on the floor to clean, and tears to dry on sad little faces. I wouldn't trade any of it for all the money in the world. Loving my bride and our four kiddos (and now 15 grandkids) has been the "banana split and whipped cream" of my life.

It's easy to fall in love, but only solidly developed character can *keep* love alive. It's easy to have a wedding, but only two hearts sold out to following Jesus can have a "First Corinthians 13" *marriage*. It's easy to have a child, but only through the consistent modeling of a life devoted to godly living can you *raise* a Christian leader. It's easy to build a house, but only God can build a *home*. Unfortunately, most marriages in America either fail or live unhappily together. Most homes fall apart far sooner than the intended purpose of that home has been fulfilled. The vast majority of American children give in to porn, sex, alcohol, and drugs during their teenage years. But children who are discipled in a solid home are far less likely to fall into and stay in these lifestyles of sin.

So *how* does God build a home? *When* does that process begin? *What* are the necessary steps taken along the way?

How?	A God-built home begins with a man and a woman who have *died* to themselves and are committed to *live* in *staunchly* moral integrity.
When?	Whether you're 16 or 26 or 86, the answer is NOW. Literally every decision you make, honest or dishonest, moral or impure, selfish or unselfish; every choice of attitude, thought, and deed—these are the nails and 2 x 4 lumber you will have to build your home, be it weak or strong.
How?	A godly, unbreakable home requires a man and a woman who go to God daily for wisdom, choose purity over porn, put *God* first rather than *me* first, think *What can I give?* over *What can I take?*, choose the substance of the Word over artificial stimulants, and prefer honesty to hypocrisy.

Yes, it's hard to build a *good home*. It's difficult to have a *good marriage*. It's rare to have a *godly family*. But to those willing to sacrifice for them, they are the crown jewels of life.

1) **Ephesians 5:25** - *"Husbands, love your wives, just as Christ also loved the church and gave Himself up for her."*

   What does it mean to you *today* (single or married) to love your spouse (whether you've met her or him or not) as Christ loves the church?

   _____

   _____

2) **1 Corinthians 6:19-20** - *"Or do you not know that your body is a temple of the Holy Spirit who is in you, whom you have from God, and that you are not your own? For you have been bought with a price: therefore glorify God in your body."*

   1 Corinthians 7:3-4 - *"The husband must fulfill his duty to his wife, and likewise also the wife to her husband. The wife does not have authority over her own body, but the husband does; and likewise also the husband does not have authority over his own body, but the wife does."*

   What do these scriptures say to you about the moral decisions you make with your eyes, ears, and body?

   _____

   _____

3) **1 Corinthians 11:1** - *"Be imitators of me, just as I also am of Christ."*

   Since the greatest sermon you preach to your spouse and children is how you live your life, and your legacy with your family is the picture of how you live your life, what values and standards do you need to establish to build a godly home?

   _____

   _____

4) **1 Timothy 5:8** - *"But if anyone does not provide for his own, and especially for those of his household, he has denied the faith and is worse than an unbeliever."*

   Acts 10:2 - *"A devout man and one who feared God with all his household, and gave many alms to the Jewish people and prayed to God continually."*

   Ephesians 6:4 - *"Fathers, do not provoke your children to anger, but bring them up in the discipline and instruction of the Lord."*

   Colossians 3:13 - *"Bearing with one another, and forgiving each other, whoever has a complaint against anyone; just as the Lord forgave you, so also should you."*

What tools do you see in these passages that are useful in building a godly home?

_____

_____

5) **Psalm 127:3-5** - _"Behold, children are a gift of the Lord, the fruit of the womb is a reward. Like arrows in the hand of a warrior, so are the children of one's youth. How blessed is the man whose quiver is full of them; they will not be ashamed when they speak with their enemies in the gate."_

Proverbs 15:20 - _"A wise son makes a father glad, but a foolish man despises his mother."_

What kind of a man or woman do you need to be _today_ to raise godly children _tomorrow_? What changes do you need to make _now_ in the way you're living?

_____

_____

THE SHEPHERD'S CALL

6) **John 13:15** - _"For I gave you an example that you also should do as I did to you."_

From today's scripture, how does **THE** Shepherd inspire **you** to shepherd **your** flock?

_____

_____

MINUTE OF MEDITATION

"Bearing with one another, and forgiving each other, whoever has a complaint against anyone; just as the Lord forgave you, so also should you"
(Colossians 3:13).

PRAYER

Adoration, **C**onfession, **T**hanksgiving, **S**upplication

<u>To Wait on the Lord</u>

"I wait for the Lord, my soul does wait, and in His word do I hope. My soul waits for the Lord more than the watchmen for the morning; indeed, more than the watchmen for the morning" (Psalm 130:5-6).

Psalm 130

Instant coffee, instant microwave cooking, instant Amazon delivery, instant drive-through burgers and fries, instant vacation reservations, instant answers from Google, instant gratification on the Internet. You want to sell something to 21st-century Americans? Make it easy, quick, and cheap.

Perhaps that's why 13 million microwave ovens were sold in America last year, a staggering 50 billion hamburgers were consumed, $83 billion were spent on beer, and $80 billion were spent on the lottery. Oh, and an estimated $13 billion were spent on porn, costing American business productivity $16.9 billion by its use while on the job.

In this "insta" world where we now live, why would anyone want to *wait* on God? To wait on the Lord is to set aside *your* skills, *your* talents, *your* gifts, and most importantly *your* timetable in exchange for *His* resources and *His* timing. To wait on the Lord is to trust and hope expectantly for His answers, His results, and His perspective.

Isaiah 40:31 proclaims, *"Yet those who wait for the Lord will gain new strength; they will mount up with wings like eagles, they will run and not get tired, they will walk and not become weary."*

If we wait on the Lord, He will renew our strength. We will be raised *above* our problems. We will be provided with greater rewards; receive greater fulfillment and satisfaction in life; experience deeper and longer-lasting relationships; live life more richly; worry, fear, and stress less; and enjoy a bit of heaven even before we arrive!

"Lead me in Your truth and teach me, for You are the God of my salvation; for You I wait all the day" (Psalm 25:5).

1) **Micah** 7:7 - *"But as for me, I will watch expectantly for the Lord; I will wait for the God of my salvation. My God will hear me."*

   What does it mean to you to wait on the Lord?

   _____

   _____

2) **Psalm 33:20** - *"Our soul waits for the Lord; He is our help and our shield."*

   Psalm 130:5 - *"I wait for the Lord, my soul does wait, and in His word do I hope."*

   How can you overcome impulsiveness and self-seeking so you can wait on the Lord?

   _____

   _____

3) **Hebrews 9:28** - *"So Christ also, having been offered once to bear the sins of many, will appear a second time for salvation without reference to sin, to those who eagerly await Him."*

   James 5:7-8 - *"Therefore be patient, brethren, until the coming of the Lord. The farmer waits for the precious produce of the soil, being patient about it, until it gets the early and late rains. You too be patient; strengthen your hearts, for the coming of the Lord is near."*

   How does waiting on the Lord apply to anticipating Jesus' second coming?

   _____

   _____

4) **Luke 12:35-40** - *"Be dressed in readiness, and keep your lamps lit. Be like men who are waiting for their master when he returns from the wedding feast, so that they may immediately open the door to him when he comes and knocks. Blessed are those slaves whom the master will find on the alert when he comes; truly I say to you, that he will gird himself to serve, and have them recline at the table, and will come up and wait on them. Whether he comes in the second watch, or even in the third, and finds them so, blessed are those slaves. But be sure of this, that if the head of the house had known at what hour the thief was coming, he would not have allowed his house to be broken into. You too, be ready; for the Son of Man is coming at an hour that you do not expect."*

   What does Jesus ask from you as you wait on His coming?

   _____

   _____

   In practical ways, how do you stay "on the alert" for His return?

   _____

   _____

THE SHEPHERD'S CALL

5) **John 13:15** - *"For I gave you an example that you also should do as I did to you."*

   From today's scripture, how does **THE** Shepherd inspire **you** to shepherd **your** flock?

   _____

   _____

MINUTE OF MEDITATION
"I wait for the Lord, my soul does wait, and in His word do I hope"
(Psalm 130:5).

PRAYER
Adoration, **C**onfession, **T**hanksgiving, **S**upplication

Accountability

"Behold, how good and how pleasant it is for brothers to dwell together in unity" (Psalm 133:1).

Psalm 133

On December 22, 1944, at approximately 11:30 A.M., four German soldiers waving two white peace flags approached General Anthony McAuliffe, senior commanding officer of the U.S. 101st Airborne Division, who had just secured the town of Bastogne, Belgium, during the pivotal Battle of the Bulge in the closing days of World War II.

The following note was given to the American commander from German General Heinrich Freiherr von Lüttwitz as 54,000 soldiers from seven divisions of the German army surrounded the highly outnumbered 101st Airborne, with its 11,000 "nitty gritty" fighting soldiers, and only 11,000 other American fighters:

To the U.S.A. Commander of the encircled town of Bastogne.

The fortune of war is changing. This time the U.S.A. forces in and near Bastogne have been encircled by strong German armored units. More German armored units have crossed the river Our near Ortheuville, have taken Marche and reached St. Hubert by passing through Hompre-Sibret-Tillet. Libramont is in German hands.

There is only one possibility to save the encircled U.S.A. troops from total annihilation: that is the honorable surrender of the encircled town. In order to think it over a term of two hours will be granted beginning with the presentation of this note.

If this proposal should be rejected one German artillery corps and six heavy A. A. battalions are ready to annihilate the U.S.A. troops in and near Bastogne. The order for firing will be given immediately after this two hours term.

Signed,
The German Commander.

Upon reading the note, the salty, veteran U.S. general staunchly replied, "Nuts! ... U.S. surrender? Aw nuts."

The severe battle that followed was not without casualties, but the 101st prevailed with the help of reinforcements and won a decisive victory. The success of the 101st in that battle was pivotal to the final defeat of the German tyranny and Allied victory in World War II.

The Germans greatly underestimated the strategic power of teamwork, as it had been demonstrated again and again by the 101st "Screaming Eagles" since its inception in 1918 at Camp Shelby, Mississippi.

The division's first commander, Major General William Coler, commissioned the 101st with these prophetic words: "Each individual, each officer, each enlisted man must regard himself as a necessary part of a complex and powerful instrument for the overcoming of the enemies of our nation."

As it is in wars with guns and tanks, so it is in the spiritual battles every man and woman face every day of their lives. The power of *team* wins wars. The power of *team* defeats Satan, the archenemy of God.

1) **Proverbs 27:17** - *"Iron sharpens iron, so one man sharpens another."* How does an honest accountability relationship help us to overcome sin?

   _____

   _____

2) **Hebrews 10:24-25** - *"And let us consider how to stimulate one another to love and good deeds, not forsaking our own assembling together, as is the habit of some, but encouraging one another; and all the more as you see the day drawing near."*

   According to this passage, what vital contribution does teamwork make to the fulfilling of your mission from Jesus?

   _____

   _____

3) **Ecclesiastes 4:9-12** - *"Two are better than one because they have a good return for their labor. For if either of them falls, the one will lift up his companion. But woe to the one who falls when there is not another to lift him up. Furthermore, if two lie down together they keep warm, but how can one be warm alone? And if one can overpower him who is alone, two can resist him. A cord of three strands is not quickly torn apart."*

   Galatians 2:20 - *"I have been crucified with Christ; and it is no longer I who live, but Christ lives in me; and the life which I now live in the flesh I live by faith in the Son of God, who loved me and gave Himself up for me."*

   How can you develop a godly team around you?

   _____

   _____

   What do you need to do to become a better team player yourself?

   _____

   _____

4) **Proverbs 11:14** - *"Where there is no guidance the people fall, but in abundance of counselors there is victory."*

Why must you always keep submitting yourself to a strong team of believers?

_____

_____

5) **Romans 15:5-6** - *"Now may the God who gives perseverance and encouragement grant you to be of the same mind with one another according to Christ Jesus, so that with one accord you may with one voice glorify the God and Father of our Lord Jesus Christ."*

A team bound together by the Holy Spirit for the cause of making Jesus known to the world is the strongest band of foot soldiers ever assembled. Do you have such a team around you? If not, what steps can you take, starting today, to begin building it?

_____

_____

6) **1 John 1:7** - *"But if we walk in the Light as He Himself is in the Light, we have fellowship with one another, and the blood of Jesus His Son cleanses us from all sin."*

Why is "walking in the Light" essential for building a team?

_____

_____

THE SHEPHERD'S CALL

7) **John 13:15** - *"For I gave you an example that you also should do as I did to you."*

From today's scripture, how does **THE** Shepherd inspire **you** to shepherd **your** flock?

_____

_____

MINUTE OF MEDITATION
"Behold, how good and how pleasant it is for brothers to dwell together in unity" (Psalm 133:1).

PRAYER
Adoration, **C**onfession, **T**hanksgiving, **S**upplication

<u>Certainty</u>

"For I know that the Lord is great and that our Lord is above all gods. Whatever the Lord pleases, He does, in heaven and in earth, in the seas and in all deeps" (Psalm 135:5-6).

Psalm 135

What are your "positives?"

Either God exists or He doesn't.
Yes   No

Either God is the cosmos creator or He's not.
Yes   No

Either He is sovereign or He's not.
Yes   No

Either His word is accurate or it's not.
Yes   No

Either Jesus came to the earth as God's only Son or He didn't.
Yes   No

Either He was crucified or He wasn't.
Yes   No

Either His crucifixion was necessary to save us from hell or it wasn't.
Yes   No

Either He was resurrected from the dead or He wasn't.
Yes   No

Either faith in Jesus provides eternal life for sincere believers or it doesn't.
Yes   No

Either Jesus is your Lord or He isn't.
Yes   No

"No one can serve two masters; for either he will hate the one and love the other, or he will be devoted to one and despise the other. You cannot serve God and wealth" (Matthew 6:24).

During the Roman imprisonment of the apostle Paul, the conditions must have been horrible and his living conditions deplorable. Compared to the living standards we enjoy today, even the life of an average man living in freedom in that day was hard during the best of times.

For Paul, with his body beaten by whips, rods, and stones many times over and then chained to a Roman guard in his tiny area of confinement, his circumstances must have been dire. The ridicule of the Roman guard was inevitable, and yet Paul's foundation was firm and sound: *"For this reason I also suffer these things, but I am not ashamed; for I know whom I have believed and I am convinced that He is able to guard what I have entrusted to Him until that day"* (2 Timothy 1:12).

He was *positive* that God created him; that Jesus, God's Son, had been sent to forgive his sins; and that Jesus' resurrection was real and true. Paul's *certainty* of God's sovereign, graceful existence made his earthly conditions "momentary and light afflictions."

Knowing God with *unwavering* faith yields perseverance. Knowing God with *unshakable* character yields perseverance. And best of all, knowing God with *unquestionable* hope yields perseverance.

1) **2 Chronicles 20:6** - *"And he said, "O Lord, the God of our fathers, are You not God in the heavens? And are You not ruler over all the kingdoms of the nations? Power and might are in Your hand so that no one can stand against You."*

   Job 40:2 - *"Will the faultfinder contend with the Almighty? Let him who reproves God answer it."*

   How did you answer the yes or no choices (your "positives") in the quiz above?

   _____

   _____

   What do these passages tell you about the source of courage? If God is all-powerful and your faith is unwavering, how much more courageous should you be? How true is that of you today?

   _____

   _____

2) **Psalm 111:6** - *"He has made known to His people the power of His works, in giving them the heritage of the nations."*

   Psalm 56:11 - *"In God I have put my trust, I shall not be afraid. What can man do to me?"*

   What is your greatest fear? What impact do these passages have on your fear?

   _____

   _____

3) **Revelation 15:3** - *"Great and marvelous are Your works, O Lord God, the Almighty; righteous and true are Your ways, King of the nations!"* How do your "positives" influence your moral decisions and integrity issues?

   _____

   _____

4) **1 Chronicles 29:11** - *"Yours, O Lord, is the greatness and the power and the glory and the victory and the majesty, indeed everything that is in the heavens and the earth; Yours is the dominion, O Lord, and You exalt Yourself as head over all."*

If you believe the words of this passage, how should your prayer life and Scripture-seeking life be different?
_____
_____

5) **Hebrews 12:1-2** - *"Therefore, since we have so great a cloud of witnesses surrounding us, let us also lay aside every encumbrance and the sin which so easily entangles us, and let us run with endurance the race that is set before us, fixing our eyes on Jesus, the author and perfecter of faith, who for the joy set before Him endured the cross, despising the shame, and has sat down at the right hand of the throne of God."*

As Jesus lived to reflect God's sovereign goodness, how should you live? How should Jesus' staunch commitment to His purpose influence yours?
_____
_____

THE SHEPHERD'S CALL
6) **John 13:15** - *"For I gave you an example that you also should do as I did to you."*

From today's scripture, how does **THE** Shepherd inspire **you** to shepherd **your** flock?
_____
_____

MINUTE OF MEDITATION
"For I know that the Lord is great and that our Lord is above all gods. Whatever the Lord pleases, He does, in heaven and in earth, in the seas and in all deeps" (Psalm 135:5-6).

PRAYER
Adoration, **C**onfession, **T**hanksgiving, **S**upplication

Remembering God's Goodness

"If I forget you, O Jerusalem, may my right hand forget her skill. May my tongue cling to the roof of my mouth if I do not remember you, if I do not exalt Jerusalem above my chief joy" (Psalm 137:5-6).

Psalm 137

"What have you done for me *lately*?" This is the cry of entitlement. This is the trademark of ingratitude. This is the motto of the one who loves God's hands, not His heart. This is the person who sees God as a vending machine, not a person to be loved, admired, and followed.

In many ways, the history of Israel is the pattern for life in the church today. As the Jews *anticipated* the Messiah, so we *worship* the Messiah. As they prophesied *of* the Messiah's coming, so we rejoice *in* His coming. As they rebelled as a nation, so we rebel as individuals. As they received discipline for their rebellion, so we are disciplined for ours. As they took for granted their blessings, so do we.

But the Hebrew people did one thing that we, as followers of Jesus, should be much more disciplined to emulate. The Hebrew nation wrote and sang about the things God had done for them with never ending fervor. The memories of the many miracles He had accomplished on their behalf were the source and vibrancy of their praise. The Hebrew people *never forgot* the God who made them, freed them, fed them, and performed mighty acts of supernatural intervention to give them their rich heritage.

Why do we as Christians forget so quickly what Jesus did for us last week, last month, last year? Why do we so often forget the moment we first trusted Him and He forgave us all our sins? Why do we whine, pout, complain, grow complacent, and rationalize and justify sinful living, allowing lukewarm commitment to continue in our lives?

Because we forget!

1) **2 Timothy 2:8** - *"Remember Jesus Christ, risen from the dead, descendant of David, according to my gospel."*

   Psalm 103:2 - *"Bless the Lord, O my soul, and forget none of His benefits."*

   How well do you make daily remembrance of God's sacrifice on your behalf? How should that memory guide you in the difficult decisions you make each day?

   _____

   _____

2) **Hebrews 8:10-12** - *"For this is the covenant that I will make with the house of Israel after those days, says the Lord: I will put My laws into their minds, and I will write them on their hearts. And I will be their God, and they shall be My people. And they shall not teach everyone his fellow citizen, and everyone his brother, saying, 'Know the Lord,' for all will know Me, from the least to the greatest of them. For I will be merciful to their iniquities, and I will remember their sins no more."*

Describe God's "selective" memory.

_____

_____

3) **John 14:26** - *"But the Helper, the Holy Spirit, whom the Father will send in My name, He will teach you all things, and bring to your remembrance all that I said to you."*

How open are you to the Holy Spirit's role in helping you remember Jesus' words? Why do you need that voice in your life?

_____

_____

4) **1 Corinthians 11:24-28** - *"And when He had given thanks, He broke it and said, 'This is My body, which is for you; do this in remembrance of Me.' In the same way He took the cup also after supper, saying, 'This cup is the new covenant in My blood; do this, as often as you drink it, in remembrance of Me.' For as often as you eat this bread and drink the cup, you proclaim the Lord's death until He comes. Therefore whoever eats the bread or drinks the cup of the Lord in an unworthy manner, shall be guilty of the body and the blood of the Lord. But a man must examine himself, and in so doing he is to eat of the bread and drink of the cup."*

According to this passage, what's the purpose of taking the covenant meal (Communion) on a regular basis in a place of worship?

_____

_____

5) **2 Peter 1:5-9** - *"Now for this very reason also, applying all diligence, in your faith supply moral excellence, and in your moral excellence, knowledge, and in your knowledge, self-control, and in your self-control, perseverance, and in your perseverance, godliness, and in your godliness, brotherly kindness, and in your brotherly kindness, love. For if these qualities are yours and are increasing, they render you neither useless nor unfruitful in the true knowledge of our Lord Jesus Christ. For he who lacks these qualities is blind or short-sighted, having forgotten his purification from his former sins."*

Why is remembering the gift of God's grace so motivating for a wholehearted pursuit of godly living?

_____

_____

Why is forgetting Jesus' sacrifice the root of purposeless living?

_____

_____

6) **Philippians 3:13-14** - *"Brethren, I do not regard myself as having laid hold of it yet; but one thing I do: forgetting what lies behind and reaching forward to what lies ahead, I press on toward the goal for the prize of the upward call of God in Christ Jesus."*

Ephesians 4:32 - *"Be kind to one another, tender-hearted, forgiving each other, just as God in Christ also has forgiven you."*
When is forgetting a good idea?

_____

_____

THE SHEPHERD'S CALL
7) **John 13:15** - *"For I gave you an example that you also should do as I did to you."*

From today's scripture, how does **THE** Shepherd inspire **you** to shepherd **your** flock?

_____

_____

MINUTE OF MEDITATION
"If I forget you, O Jerusalem, may my right hand forget her skill. May my tongue cling to the roof of my mouth if I do not remember you, if I do not exalt Jerusalem above my chief joy" (Psalm 137:5-6).

PRAYER
Adoration, **C**onfession, **T**hanksgiving, **S**upplication

An Attitude of Gratitude

"I will give You thanks with all my heart" (Psalm 138:1a).

Psalm 138

In the brilliant book *The HeartMath Solution*, by Doc Lew Childre and Howard Martin, endorsed by many doctors and psychologists alike, the case is made for the emotional and intellectual influence of the human heart. The book asserts that your mood, your demeanor, your attitude, your words, and your actions are dependent on whether you are controlled by your brain or your heart. Your heart, research shows, is the source of grace, peace, tenderness, kindness, and love. Your brain, in contrast, is the source of anger, bitterness, unkindness, and fear. The book claims that you can "amp up" your heart by being thankful. In the same way you plug in your smartphone at night, you can plug in and recharge your heart by maintaining an attitude of gratitude, and you will then be known as a man or woman of grace rather than a man or woman of fear.

In the summer of 2018, *Time* magazine did an exhaustive study titled "The Science of Happiness." The magazine came to the same conclusion. Happy people are thankful people.

Thankfulness and *happiness* are synonyms. *Gloominess* and *entitlement* are likewise synonyms. First Thessalonians 5:18 exhorts, *"In everything give thanks; for this is God's will for you in Christ Jesus."* There is no poem, no song, no sonnet, no story, no theatrical script more beautifully written on the subject of thanksgiving than Psalm 138.

In this psalm (essential to memorize and meditate on regularly), God is appreciated for His lovingkindness, His provision, His sovereignty, His greatness, His glory, His regard for the meek, His help in times of trouble, His salvation, His willingness to accomplish our greatest concerns, and His everlasting love.

1) **Psalm 138:2** - *"I will bow down toward Your holy temple and give thanks to Your name for Your lovingkindness and Your truth; for You have magnified Your word according to all Your name."*

   Lovingkindness is God's love demonstrated by what He has done for us. Our response should be unbridled thanksgiving. How well does your heart respond to His lovingkindness?
   _____
   _____

2) **Psalm 138:3** - *"On the day I called, You answered me; You made me bold with strength in my soul."*

   Do you believe God is attentive to your prayers? Why or why not? How does this affect your level of thankfulness?
   _____
   _____

3) **Psalm 138:7-8** - *"Though I walk in the midst of trouble, You will revive me; You will stretch forth Your hand against the wrath of my enemies, and Your right hand will save me. The Lord will accomplish what concerns me; Your lovingkindness, O Lord, is everlasting; do not forsake the works of Your hands."*

List three to five things God does that make you thankful.

_____

_____

4) **Philippians 4:6** - *"Be anxious for nothing, but in everything by prayer and supplication with thanksgiving let your requests be made known to God."*

Why does thanksgiving eradicate worry and fear?

_____

_____

5) **2 Chronicles 5:13** - *"In unison when the trumpeters and the singers were to make themselves heard with one voice to praise and to glorify the Lord, and when they lifted up their voice accompanied by trumpets and cymbals and instruments of music, and when they praised the Lord saying, 'He indeed is good for His lovingkindness is everlasting,' then the house, the house of the Lord, was filled with a cloud."*

What has God done for you that deserves trumpets, cymbals, orchestras, and singers? In practical ways, what can you do in your daily life to bring "the orchestra of thanksgiving" to Him?

_____

_____

THE SHEPHERD'S CALL
6) **John 13:15** - *"For I gave you an example that you also should do as I did to you."*

From today's scripture, how does **THE** Shepherd inspire **you** to shepherd **your** flock?

_____

_____

MINUTE OF MEDITATION
"On the day I called, You answered me; You made me bold with strength in my soul" (Psalm 138:3).

PRAYER
Adoration, **C**onfession, **T**hanksgiving, **S**upplication

Selah

"How precious also are Your thoughts to me, O God! How vast is the sum of them! If I should count them, they would outnumber the sand. When I awake, I am still with You" (Psalm 139:17-18).

Psalm 139

From time to time as you read the psalms, you come upon a curious word: "Selah." (No, it's not a girl's name!) It means to pause, to take a breath, to soak it in, to slow down and let the truth touch your soul.

The One who knows you best, loves you most.
Take a deep breath … *Selah.*
Let that thought sink in for a minute.
The One who knows you best, loves you most.
Selah.

This is the case for Psalm 139. Perhaps in no other place in all of Scripture do you find such a treatise of intimacy. This beloved psalm must have come to David's mind *in the eye of a hurricane*. David had as many hurricanes in his world as the Caribbean has between June and November. As soon as one storm passes, another is just on its heels. In the Atlantic Ocean during one hurricane season, there are as many as 16 named storms, many of which develop into full-force hurricanes. For David, the hurricane season lasted 12 months each year. Perhaps you can relate.

Our family had a friend who chased hurricanes for a living; probably not the dream job for every aspiring young pilot! Our friend's job was to fly into the eye of the hurricane and gather data for the weather forecasters below, whose job was to make accurate predictions of the storm's path and strength. Though I was just a young lad when I met that pilot, I will never forget his description of the eye of the hurricane and how peaceful and calm it was in the middle of such a violent storm.

Have you ever longed for an "eye in your hurricane"? Psalm 139 is exactly that. You can "fly into the eye" any time you choose as you meditate on the life-giving words of David.

Selah.

Don't rush through the eye of this storm. Memorize it. Meditate on it often. There is emotional healing and emotional intimacy with the Shepherd as you allow the Holy Spirit to transfer these tender words from your mind to your heart.

1) **Psalm 139:1-2 -** *"O Lord, You have searched me and known me. You know when I sit down and when I rise up; You understand my thought from afar."*

Jeremiah 1:5 - *"Before I formed you in the womb I knew you, and before you were born I consecrated you; I have appointed you a prophet to the nations."*

The Hebrew word for *know* here is *Yada*, which means "to clearly understand," "familiar friend," "chosen," "regard," "understand," "know well." *Yada* between God and one of His followers is a covenant term that indicates "a relationship that cannot be broken." Back to the beginning of this study: "The One who knows you best, loves you most." What does it mean to you to be known by God in this regard?

_____

_____

2) **Psalm 134:3 -** *"May the Lord bless you from Zion, He who made heaven and earth."*

John 17:3 - *"This is eternal life, that they may know You, the only true God, and Jesus Christ whom You have sent."*

In the marriage covenant between man and wife, to intimately know is to "become one flesh" emotionally, spiritually, physically, and socially. In a Christ-centered marriage, the more intimacy you know, the more you love. The longer you know, the more you love. With God it goes so much deeper! It is eternal knowledge. It's never ending love. It's love with no bounds; love without limits. In Ephesians 3:18, Paul prays that we might know *"the breadth and length and height and depth"* of God's love. How do you describe God's "intimate love" for you?

_____

_____

How should living in the moment-by-moment knowledge of that love change the way you think and the way you live?

_____

_____

3) **Psalm 139:4-6 -** *"Even before there is a word on my tongue, behold, O Lord, You know it all. You have enclosed me behind and before, and laid Your hand upon me. Such knowledge is too wonderful for me; it is too high, I cannot attain to it."*

What is David feeling as he says, "Such knowledge is too wonderful for me; it is too high, I cannot attain to it"?

_____

_____

4) **Psalm 139:7-10** - *"Where can I go from Your Spirit? Or where can I flee from Your presence? If I ascend to heaven, You are there; if I make my bed in Sheol, behold, You are there. If I take the wings of the dawn, if I dwell in the remotest part of the sea, even there Your hand will lead me, and Your right hand will lay hold of me."*

Describe a time you found yourself in the "remotest part of the sea." What was it like when God "found you there" and you were seized by His right hand of blessing?

_____

_____

5) **Psalm 139:11-12** - *"If I say, 'Surely the darkness will overwhelm me, and the light around me will be night,' even the darkness is not dark to You, and the night is as bright as the day. Darkness and light are alike to You."*

John 8:12 - *"Then Jesus again spoke to them, saying, 'I am the Light of the world; he who follows Me will not walk in the darkness, but will have the Light of life.'"*

If Jesus lives in your heart, what are these two passages telling you?

_____

_____

6) **Psalm 139:16-18** - *"Your eyes have seen my unformed substance; and in Your book were all written the days that were ordained for me, when as yet there was not one of them. How precious also are Your thoughts to me, O God! How vast is the sum of them! If I should count them, they would outnumber the sand. When I awake, I am still with You."*

When you get down on yourself, pick on yourself, and point out your failures and weaknesses in your thought life, what would Psalm 139 suggest you do with those thoughts?

_____

_____

How should you view yourself in the light of Psalm 139?

_____

_____

THE SHEPHERD'S CALL

7) **John 13:15** - *"For I gave you an example that you also should do as I did to you."*

From today's scripture, how does **THE** Shepherd inspire **you** to shepherd **your** flock?

_____

_____

278

MINUTE OF MEDITATION

"How precious also are Your thoughts to me, O God! How vast is the sum of them! If I should count them, they would outnumber the sand. When I awake, I am still with You" (Psalm 139:17-18).

PRAYER

Adoration, **C**onfession, **T**hanksgiving, **S**upplication

The Cry of the Lamb

"Do not grant, O Lord, the desires of the wicked; do not promote his evil device, that they not be exalted. Selah. As for the head of those who surround me, may the mischief of their lips cover them" (Psalm 140:8-9).

Psalm 140

"Do not lead us into temptation, but deliver us from evil" (Matthew 6:13). In this most-well-known prayer from around the world, Jesus gives His followers the stark realization that only "the Great Shepherd of the Sheep" can protect His lambs from the snare of the enemy. Only "the Great Shepherd of the Sheep" can empower a follower to overcome sin. Only "the Great Shepherd of the Sheep" can build a heart that is blameless, without a spot or blemish; a mind that thinks pure thoughts; a mouth that utters consistent words of honor; and a soul that can be maintained respectfully.

In a foreshadowing of the great Lord's Prayer from the Sermon on the Mount, David breaks out with "the Cry of the Lamb" in Psalm 140:1-4: *"Rescue me, O Lord, from evil men; preserve me from violent men who devise evil things in their hearts; they continually stir up wars. They sharpen their tongues as a serpent; poison of a viper is under their lips. Selah. Keep me, O Lord, from the hands of the wicked; preserve me from violent men who have purposed to trip up my feet."*

Jesus knew full well that Satan came only to *"steal and kill and destroy"* (John 10:10), that the enemy's voice speaks only evil lies continuously; that the lamb is helpless before him without God's hand of protection. So He told us to pray like David and acknowledge God's sole authority to provide and protect.

1) **Exodus 14:13-14** - *"But Moses said to the people, 'Do not fear! Stand by and see the salvation of the Lord which He will accomplish for you today; for the Egyptians whom you have seen today, you will never see them again forever. The Lord will fight for you while you keep silent.'"*

   What is Moses saying to you today?

   _____

   _____

2) **2 Samuel 22:3-4** - *"My God, my rock, in whom I take refuge, my shield and the horn of my salvation, my stronghold and my refuge; my savior, You save me from violence. I call upon the Lord, who is worthy to be praised, and I am saved from my enemies."*

   Describe a time when you went to other sources looking for spiritual and/or emotional protection. Where did you turn? What did you learn?

   _____

   _____

When did you learn to cry out to God for protection? How were you made aware that He and only He could protect you from evil?

_____

_____

3) **Psalm 34:19** - *"Many are the afflictions of the righteous, but the Lord delivers him out of them all."*

   Proverbs 18:10 - *"The name of the Lord is a strong tower; the righteous runs into it and is safe."*

   How do you relate to David and Solomon in passages such as these?

   _____

   _____

4) **Nahum 1:7** - *"The Lord is good, a stronghold in the day of trouble, and He knows those who take refuge in Him."*

   Zephaniah 3:17 - *"The Lord your God is in your midst, a victorious warrior. He will exult over you with joy, He will be quiet in His love, He will rejoice over you with shouts of joy."*

   What does it mean to you to know He is your protector?

   _____

   _____

   When is it difficult for you to trust Him alone for protection? Why?

   _____

   _____

5) **2 Corinthians 4:8-9** - *"We are afflicted in every way, but not crushed; perplexed, but not despairing; persecuted, but not forsaken; struck down, but not destroyed."*

   Ephesians 6:13 - *"Therefore, take up the full armor of God, so that you will be able to resist in the evil day, and having done everything, to stand firm."*

   What would you say to a friend who is feeling persecuted by the enemy?

   _____

   _____

THE SHEPHERD'S CALL

6) **John 13:15** - *"For I gave you an example that you also should do as I did to you."*

   From today's scripture, how does **THE** Shepherd inspire **you** to shepherd **your** flock?

   _____

   _____

MINUTE OF MEDITATION

"The name of the Lord is a strong tower; the righteous runs into it and is safe" (Proverbs 18:10).

PRAYER

Adoration, Confession, Thanksgiving, Supplication

Desperation

"For the enemy has persecuted my soul; he has crushed my life to the ground; he has made me dwell in dark places, like those who have long been dead. Therefore my spirit is overwhelmed within me; my heart is appalled within me" (Psalm 143:3-4).

Psalm 143

Brad Edgar is a dear friend who was engaged to the woman he thought he'd spend the rest of his life with. But I discovered in counseling them that her heart was in other places. The ensuing breakup was utterly painful for Brad. He literally fell apart emotionally. He lost his appetite, lost too much weight, and lost his mental rationale. His life was a wreck. In the middle of the painful wilderness, he went to the edge of a cliff to take his life.

But when he got there, he was so weak from his sufferings that he collapsed on the precipice. He literally passed out. And Jesus met him there. Together they walked away from the cliff, hand in hand, side by side. That summer I introduced him to another amazing young lady. She was and is to this day the woman of his dreams. They raised amazing children together. They do ministry together. They'll raise grandkids together. They'll be in love until the day they die.

What do *you* do when you get to the edge of the cliff?

When a friend tells you to "Run to Jesus," "Press into God," "Stand on the Rock of your faith" --all those are good advice, but how do you do it? What does it mean to "press into God" and "make Jesus your focus" when you're in lots of pain and God is *all* you've got?

In Psalm 143, David joins us in that valley and shows us how.

As I write tonight, I know firsthand the meaning and application of David's words. Early tomorrow morning, I go into the hospital for a tedious but critical surgery. The success or failure of this one has dire implications for my future quality of life. I can honestly say I have peace with God as I go in and allow the doctor to put anesthetic in my veins and "take me out" to try to save my foot from amputation.

One day you'll have a similar circumstance, if you haven't been there already. Take heed as you study David's inspiring words. They work. I've been there before. Tomorrow I'll go there again.

"I remember the days of old; I meditate on all Your doings; I muse on the work of Your hands. I stretch out my hands to You; my soul longs for You, as a parched land" (Psalm 143:5-6.

Read each word carefully, thoughtfully, and reflectively as you begin to absorb David's five habits for living faithfully in the pit of despair.

1. *Remember* gratefully God's goodness.
2. *Meditate* on His Word.
3. *Muse* (gaze thoughtfully).
4. *Stretch out* your hands and surrender.
5. *Long* for God deeply.

1) **Remember**
   Deuteronomy 5:15 - *"You shall remember that you were a slave in the land of Egypt, and the Lord your God brought you out of there by a mighty hand and by an outstretched arm; therefore the Lord your God commanded you to observe the sabbath day."*

   For the Jewish people, remembering all God had done for them gave them hope. That hope was effective in helping them overcome their times of despair. If you were going to make a list of all the favors, benefits, and freedoms God has granted you, which three events would be at the top of the list?

   _____

   _____

2) **Meditate**
   Isaiah 26:3 - *"The steadfast of mind You will keep in perfect peace, because he trusts in You."*

   Why does meditation on God's memorized Word bring peace and comfort?

   _____

   _____

3) **Muse**
   Psalm 86:10 - *"For You are great and do wondrous deeds; You alone are God."*

   Psalm 118:23 - *"This is the Lord's doing; it is marvelous in our eyes."* *Muse* means *inspiration*: a person who is the source of inspiration for a creative artist.

   To muse on God means to stand in sheer awe, wonder, and amazement over who He is and all He has done. Why does that kind of mental activity help alleviate depression?

   _____

   _____

4) **Stretch out**
   Psalm 28:2 - *"Hear the voice of my supplications when I cry to You for help, when I lift up my hands toward Your holy sanctuary."*

   Psalm 63:1 - *"O God, You are my God; I shall seek you earnestly; my soul thirsts for You, my flesh yearns for you, in a dry and weary land where there is no water."*

   When was the last time you were at the end of yourself and you stretched your arms upward fully and said, "God, I can't do this alone; I need You to save me; I need You to comfort me"?

   _____

   _____

5) **Longing**

Psalm 73:25 - *"Whom have I in heaven but You? And besides You, I desire nothing on earth."*

Isaiah 26:9 - *"At night my soul longs for You, indeed, my spirit within me seeks You diligently; for when the earth experiences Your judgments the inhabitants of the world learn righteousness."*

Describe your soul when it longs for God.

_____

_____

How does longing for God, remembering His goodness, musing in amazement, meditating on His Word, and stretching open hands to Him fight against and help overcome desperation?

_____

_____

THE SHEPHERD'S CALL

6) **John 13:15** - *"For I gave you an example that you also should do as I did to you."*

From today's scripture, how does **THE** Shepherd inspire **you** to shepherd **your** flock?

_____

_____

MINUTE OF MEDITATION

"The steadfast of mind You will keep in perfect peace, because he trusts in You" (Isaiah 26:3).

PRAYER

Adoration, **C**onfession, **T**hanksgiving, **S**upplication

Sheer Amazement

"O Lord, what is man, that You take knowledge of him? Or the son of man, that You think of him? Man is like a mere breath; his days are like a passing shadow" (Psalm 144:3-4).

Psalm 144

From the vantage point of a space traveler orbiting our moon 235,000 miles from the earth, our planet is a beautiful sight to behold! But viewing our planetary home from our sun is a bit less impressive. From that vantage point, only 93 million miles away, planet earth is only a shiny, blue dot in a vast, starry sky. But if you travel only 4.2 light years to our nearest star system, Alpha Centauri, the earth is invisible to the naked eye. From that point of view, the small, blue dot in the cosmos has completely vanished. In terms of cosmic vastness and architectural structure, our planet is less significant than a grain of sand on an endless ocean beach.

David, the stargazing shepherd, was well acquainted with the sky above and understood the dilemma. How can the One big enough to deliver the cosmos out of a mere thought in His mind actually care for an extremely small and insignificant blue dot and the tiny creatures who inhabit that planet?

Our Creator can indeed create not only lightning and thunder, hurricanes and continent-shifting earthquakes, with a blink of His eye, but He can also create entire star systems and solar systems with a simple thought in His immeasurably vast imagination.

So who is man that God would actually care *about* him, care *for* him, and *devote* Himself to him at the expense of the life of His Only Begotten Son? Sheer amazement! Staggering wonder! Awestruck admiration! Our minds can only begin to comprehend, and our words can only feebly provide an appropriate response!

1) **Psalm 144:1-2 -** *"Blessed be the Lord, my rock, who trains my hands for war, and my fingers for battle; my lovingkindness and my fortress, my stronghold and my deliverer, my shield and He in whom I take refuge, who subdues my people under me."*

   Read the words so carefully chosen! He is my *rock*. He is my *Lord*. He is the drill instructor who personally trains me for the battles I face. He makes my hands skillful in the art of self-defense. He loves me 100 percent based on what He's done for me. He is my defensive coordinator, my offensive coordinator, and the foundation upon which I put my feet and secure every step I take. What does this passage cause *you* to exclaim with wonder?

   _____

   _____

2) **Psalm 144:5-7** - *"Bow Your heavens, O Lord, and come down; touch the mountains, that they may smoke. Flash forth lightning and scatter them; send out Your arrows and confuse them. Stretch forth Your hand from on high; rescue me and deliver me out of great waters, out of the hand of aliens."*

In terms of the battles *you're* facing, what is David asking of God?

_____

_____

3) **Psalm 144:9-10** - *"I will sing a new song to You, O God; upon a harp of ten strings I will sing praises to You, who gives salvation to kings, who rescues David His servant from the evil sword."*

What was David's response to God's amazing care and hand of protection?

_____

_____

What is your level of appreciation for God's constant care, and how have you been expressing it?

_____

_____

4) **Psalm 144:15** - *"How blessed are the people who are so situated; how blessed are the people whose God is the Lord!*

What blessings are yours because God has melded your choice with His choice to place you into His very own family and make you a son or daughter of the King of the cosmos?

_____

_____

5) **Isaiah 25:1** - *"O Lord, You are my God; I will exalt You, I will give thanks to Your name; for You have worked wonders, plans formed long ago, with perfect faithfulness."*

Job 37:5 - *"God thunders with His voice wondrously, doing great things which we cannot comprehend."*

1 Chronicles 16:24 - *"Tell of His glory among the nations, His wonderful deeds among all the peoples."*

What changes in your attitudes and actions does your realization of God's greatness and personal care inspire in you?

_____

_____

THE SHEPHERD'S CALL

6) **John 13:15** - *"For I gave you an example that you also should do as I did to you."*

From today's scripture, how does **THE** Shepherd inspire **you** to shepherd **your** flock?

_____

_____

MINUTE OF MEDITATION

"Blessed be the Lord, my rock, who trains my hands for war, and my fingers for battle; my lovingkindness and my fortress, my stronghold and my deliverer, my shield and He in whom I take refuge, who subdues my people under me" (Psalm 144:1-2).

PRAYER

Adoration, **C**onfession, **T**hanksgiving, **S**upplication

Exhilaration

"Men shall speak of the power of Your awesome acts, and I will tell of Your greatness" (Psalm 145:6).

Psalm 145

To gaze into the eyes of a newborn child ... to place a wedding band on the delicate left hand of the woman you love more than you could have ever imagined possible ... to climb a 14,000-foot Colorado mountain peak and stare wondrously into the pristine nighttime sky and behold thousands of sparkling stars spanning the galaxy ... to observe a gifted artist capturing a visual wonder with astute perfection in every stroke of her brush on the canvas ... to marvel at the harmonious notes declared by an utterly synchronized orchestra of 100 stringed violins ... to scuba dive a Caribbean coral reef and behold countless multicolored fish, plants, and living rocks that span the vast aquarium below--the efforts of the imagination are endless as a God-worshipper attempts to find a comparative sight, thought, or experience that parallels the exhilaration of pure, unadulterated worship.

In Psalm 145, David tries—perhaps as in no other writing anywhere—to fathom, to behold, to stand in awe, to express the exhilaration that fills the heart, mind, and soul produced by the breadth, length, height, and depth of God's love. To memorize and meditate on this masterpiece is to reshape your heart like clay on a potter's wheel. To memorize and meditate on this incredible psalm takes you effortlessly into a zone of praise as you've never before experienced. This psalm is easily the crown jewel of worship.

1) **Psalm 145:1-2** - *"I will extol You, my God, O King, and I will bless Your name forever and ever. Every day I will bless You, and I will praise Your name forever and ever."*

   What could happen to your relationship with God if you praised Him in this manner many times throughout your day?

   _____

   _____

2) **Psalm 145:3-4** - *"Great is the Lord, and highly to be praised, and His greatness is unsearchable. One generation shall praise Your works to another, and shall declare Your mighty acts."*

   David was known as "a man after God's own heart." What thoughts and feelings toward God do the words of this psalm inspire in you?

   _____

   _____

3) **Psalm 145:5** - *"On the glorious splendor of Your majesty and on Your wonderful works, I will meditate."*

What makes daily meditation on psalms like this one so life-changing?

_____

_____

4) **Psalm 145:6-7** - *"Men shall speak of the power of Your awesome acts, and I will tell of Your greatness. They shall eagerly utter the memory of Your abundant goodness and will shout joyfully of Your righteousness."*

Do you, like David, find such thoughts of God too great to keep silent about? How freely do you express such praise? Why?

_____

_____

5) **Psalm 145: 8-13** - *"The Lord is gracious and merciful; slow to anger and great in lovingkindness. The Lord is good to all, and His mercies are over all His works. All Your works shall give thanks to You, O Lord, and Your godly ones shall bless You. They shall speak of the glory of Your kingdom and talk of Your power; to make known to the sons of men Your mighty acts and the glory of the majesty of Your kingdom. Your kingdom is an everlasting kingdom, and Your dominion endures throughout all generations."*

Describe the picture of God that you see as you meditate on this fantastic passage.

_____

_____

6) **Psalm 145:17-21** - *"The Lord is righteous in all His ways and kind in all His deeds. The Lord is near to all who call upon Him, to all who call upon Him in truth. He will fulfill the desire of those who fear Him; He will also hear their cry and will save them. The Lord keeps all who love Him, but all the wicked He will destroy. My mouth will speak the praise of the Lord, and all flesh will bless His holy name forever and ever."*

How much room is there for selfish, lustful, or other evil thoughts in a mind filled with these words of David? What conviction do they bring about your own thought life?

_____

_____

What are you willing to do to eliminate such hostile and destructive thoughts?

_____

_____

THE SHEPHERD'S CALL

7) **John 13:15** - *"For I gave you an example that you also should do as I did to you."*

From today's scripture, how does **THE** Shepherd inspire **you** to shepherd **your** flock?

_____

_____

MINUTE OF MEDITATION
"On the glorious splendor of Your majesty and on Your wonderful works, I will meditate" (Psalm 145:5).

PRAYER
Adoration, **C**onfession, **T**hanksgiving, **S**upplication

Hope

"How blessed is he whose help is the God of Jacob, whose hope is in the Lord his God" (Psalm 146:5).

Psalm 146

In his brilliant book *The Anatomy of Hope*, cancer specialist Dr. Jerome Groopman uncovers the overwhelming medicinal value of hope.

Dr. Groopman begins his study by providing his medical history. "For nearly three decades I have practiced hematology and oncology, caring for patients with cancer, blood diseases, HIV and Hepatitis C. During much of that time, at the bedside and at the laboratory bench, I failed to consider the impact of hope on any patient's illness."

Groopman continues as he zeroes in on the effect of the mysterious healing agent *hope*. "Hope is the elevating feeling we experience when we see--in the mind's eye--a path to a better future. Hope acknowledges the significant obstacles and pitfalls along the path. True hope has no room for delusion. Clear-eyed hope gives us the courage to confront our circumstances and the capacity to surmount them. For all my patients, hope, true hope, has proved as important as any medication I might prescribe or any procedure."

Billy Graham once proclaimed in one of his famous stadium crusades, "You can live for weeks without food, days without water, but you can't live a second without hope."

The apostle Paul, in his letter to the Romans, opens the eyes of our hearts toward this wonderful truth as we face tribulations and distress of all kinds: *"And not only this, but we also exult in our tribulations, knowing that tribulation brings about perseverance; and perseverance, proven character; and proven character, hope; and hope does not disappoint, because the love of God has been poured out within our hearts through the Holy Spirit who was given to us"* (Romans 5:3-5).

1) **Colossians 3:1-2** - *"Therefore if you have been raised up with Christ, keep seeking the things above, where Christ is, seated at the right hand of God. Set your mind on the things above, not on the things that are on earth."*

   Hidden in this passage is a buried treasure. Opening it provides the Christ-seeker the pathway for hope to come alive in your soul. What is that secret, and how does it inspire hope?

   _____

   _____

296

2) **Proverbs 13:12** - *"Hope deferred makes the heart sick, but desire fulfilled is a tree of life."*

   Psalm 20:7 - *"Some boast in chariots and some in horses, but we will boast in the name of the Lord, our God."*

   Why does placing your hope in people or things set you up for disappointment?

   _____

   _____

   Describe the most-memorable time in your life that you placed your hope in something (other than God) that failed you.

   _____

   _____

   What did you learn from that experience?

   _____

   _____

3) **Jeremiah 29:10-11** - *"For thus says the Lord, 'When seventy years have been completed for Babylon, I will visit you and fulfill My good word to you, to bring you back to this place. For I know the plans that I have for you,' declares the Lord, 'plans for welfare and not for calamity to give you a future and a hope.'"*

   Because of their stubbornness and their devotion to idols, God gave His people over to destruction and captivity. Yet He never gave up His desire to offer them hope. How can you relate personally to the example of the Jews in this regard?

   _____

   _____

4) **Titus 1:1-2** - *"Paul, a bondservant of God and an apostle of Jesus Christ, for the faith of those chosen of God and the knowledge of the truth which is according to godliness, in the hope of eternal life, which God, who cannot lie, promised long ages ago."*

   Titus 3:7 - *"So that being justified by His grace we would be made heirs according to the hope of eternal life."*

   Where would our hope be if Jesus had not given His life as an atonement for our sin?

   _____

   _____

   How do you place your hope in Him each day?

   _____

   _____

What qualities and acts of Jesus make Him the focus of your hope?

_____

_____

5) **Hebrews 11:1** - *"Now faith is the assurance of things hoped for, the conviction of things not seen."*

What is the relationship between faith and hope? How do faith and hope team up like peanut butter and jelly?

_____

_____

6) **1 Peter 1:3-4** - *"Blessed be the God and Father of our Lord Jesus Christ, who according to His great mercy has caused us to be born again to a living hope through the resurrection of Jesus Christ from the dead, to obtain an inheritance which is imperishable and undefiled and will not fade away, reserved in heaven for you."*

Hallelujah

Only Jesus

Prepared us for

Eternity

Where would *your* hope be without Jesus? How do His life, death, and resurrection "lock in" your hope?

_____

_____

THE SHEPHERD'S CALL

7) **John 13:15** - *"For I gave you an example that you also should do as I did to you."*

From today's scripture, how does **THE** Shepherd inspire **you** to shepherd **your** flock?

_____

_____

MINUTE OF MEDITATION
"Now faith is the assurance of things hoped for, the conviction of things not seen" (Hebrews 11:1).

PRAYER
Adoration, **C**onfession, **T**hanksgiving, **S**upplication

Infinite

"He counts the number of the stars; He gives names to all of them. Great is our Lord and abundant in strength; His understanding is infinite" (Psalm 147:4-5).

Psalm 147

Somewhat amused as I write today, I am opening a fresh, conveniently packaged Truth or Dare spearmint chewing gum box as I travel to do a student event at the University of Nebraska. As I read this amazing Psalm 147, which is fully devoted to God's infinite, overshadowing greatness and sovereignty, the sliding lid of the gum package reads in large, bold letters, "Your game, your rules." Hmm ... Pondering that for a minute: "My game, my rules." The gum's not bad ... but the philosophy? Tonight (as it is every night), as we present "The Cross" to the exuberant crowd of students, we will, by God's continually overflowing, amazing grace, see hundreds of students coming to the cross with small, white cards on which they have written "confessions to God." As we build the 12-foot cross, we will nail those cards to it in symbolism of Jesus' blood covering the countless sins that have been entrusted to His forgiving heart.

The cards are always raw and brutally honest. The burdens the students bring to the events are both sad and horrific: pornographic addition, anger, bitterness, rape, abortion, sexual sins of all kinds, degrees of degradation, lust, murder, self-mutilation, attempted suicide. The list is seemingly endless.

In concert, all the sins add up to the motto on the pack of gum I chew today, "Your game, your rules." This motto is without a doubt the call of this generation. It is a lie of lies and permeates culture as a call unto death.

In his bestselling book *The Closing of the American Mind*, Allan Bloom presents the core foundation to this tragic cultural downfall: "There is one thing that a college professor can be absolutely certain of for every incoming freshman that comes into his classroom, and that is the belief that *truth* is *relative*" (emphasis added).

In stark contrast, in this psalm the writer speaks boldly to the opposite worldview and foundation for living: "It is *God's game*. It is *God's rules*." It may not sell much gum, but my, how it springs forth fulfilling life and life eternal!

1) **Psalm 19:1** - *"The heavens are telling of the glory of God; and their expanse is declaring the work of His hands."*

Dr. Robert Jastrow, the astute founder of the Goddard Institute of NASA, said, "Now we see how the foundation of the cosmos was supernatural." A discovery by the European space agency's Planck spacecraft suggests there may be other universes, perhaps billions of them. Who knows! But the statement "God is infinite" certainly leaves that possibility open. What does the thought of God's "infinite nature" suggest about the wisdom of being fully grounded in His thinking?

_____

_____

2) **Romans 11:33** - *"Oh, the depth of the riches both of the wisdom and knowledge of God! How unsearchable are His judgments and unfathomable His ways!"*

Everlasting, immeasurable, uncontainable, omnipotent …
Select three or four more words that describe God's infinite nature. How does that realization stir your soul and motivate you to godliness?

_____

_____

3) **Ephesians 3:8** - *"To me, the very least of all saints, this grace was given, to preach to the Gentiles the unfathomable riches of Christ."*

Hebrews 1:2 - *"In these last days [God] has spoken to us in His Son, whom He appointed heir of all things, through whom also He made the world."*

John 1:1 - *"In the beginning was the Word, and the Word was with God, and the Word was God."*

The unfathomable riches of Christ in the context of God's limitlessness; what do these verses say to you about Jesus?

_____

_____

Do you feel a greater need to connect to Him more closely in light of this truth? How can you do that?

_____

_____

4) **Psalm 147:10-11** - *"He does not delight in the strength of the horse; He does not take pleasure in the legs of a man. The Lord favors those who fear Him, those who wait for His lovingkindness."*

What does this passage say about our quest for power, notoriety, fame, success, dominance, and control? What does our infinite God look for in those He favors?

_____

_____

THE SHEPHERD'S CALL
5) **John 13:15** - *"For I gave you an example that you also should do as I did to you."*

From today's scripture, how does **THE** Shepherd inspire **you** to shepherd **your** flock?

_____

_____

MINUTE OF MEDITATION
"He counts the number of the stars; He gives names to all of them. Great is our Lord and abundant in strength; His understanding is infinite"
(Psalm 147:4-5).

PRAYER
Adoration, **C**onfession, **T**hanksgiving, **S**upplication

David, a Man of Praise

"Let everything that has breath praise the Lord. Praise the Lord"
(Psalm 150:6).

Psalm 150

If you ever walk through a cemetery and read the words on the tombstones, you'll often find a short phrase that describes the life of that person. This phrase, which was labored over and pondered thoughtfully by the loved ones who placed it there, best describes and summarizes that person's life, passion, personality, purpose for living, impact, and legacy. This short phrase encapsulates the fingerprint the deceased person placed on the lives of those he or she touched in his or her brief stay on this planet.

For David, in his life as a shepherd, a warrior, a king, and a writer, the word I would place on his tombstone is *praise*. Although the Bible does not ascribe Psalm 150 to him, the theme and the writing are so consistent with the psalms we know to be his that it's reasonable to infer David might have written this one as well. And how appropriate it would be if he chose this epic psalm to finish this "Jewish hymnal," because Psalm 150 is all about praise!

Why? Because praise changes things. Praise connects the heart of the sheep to "the Heart of the Shepherd."

In the early days of contemporary Christian music, one of the headliner groups was affectionately known as The Imperials. One of their songs featured an insightful statement about praise that has stayed in my mind over the past 30 years:

"The chains that seem to bind you fall powerless
behind you when you praise the Lord!"

Praise brings freedom! Praise breaks the chains of sin, doubt, insecurity, and low self-esteem, because when you look up, you stop looking inside.

A life of praise is a life filled with joy, peace, and closeness with God. What a way to end the book of Psalms! What a way to begin to REALLY LIVE!

1) **Psalm 150:1a** - *"Praise the Lord! Praise God in His sanctuary."*

   If your body is the temple of the Holy Spirit, how do you "praise God in the sanctuary"?

   _____
   _____

2) **Psalm 150:1b-2** - *"Praise Him in His mighty expanse. Praise Him for His mighty deeds; praise Him according to His excellent greatness."*

Write down five things these verses bring to your mind about God's "mighty deeds" and "excellent greatness."

Lord, I praise you for _____

Lord, I praise you for _____

Lord, I praise you for _____

Lord, I praise you for _____

Lord, I praise you for _____

3) **Psalm 150:3-5** - *"Praise Him with trumpet sound; praise Him with harp and lyre. Praise Him with timbrel and dancing; praise Him with stringed instruments and pipe. Praise Him with loud cymbals; praise Him with resounding cymbals."*

As the Jews praised God with loud musical instruments, what means do you use today to praise the Lord?

_____

_____

4) **Psalm 150:6** - *"Let everything that has breath praise the Lord. Praise the Lord!"*

What would it look like for you to live a life of praise?

_____

_____

How would your life be different if you lived that way?

_____

_____

5) **Philippians 1:21** - *"For to me, to live is Christ and to die is gain."*

The theme of Abraham's life was "sacrificial faith," and the theme of David's life was "praise." The theme of Daniel's life was "integrity"; the theme of Paul's life was "sold out"; the theme of Peter's life was "commitment to the end"; and the theme of John's life was "a trustworthy man of vision" ... So, what theme do you want to describe your life?

_____

_____

THE SHEPHERD'S CALL

6) **John 13:15** - *"For I gave you an example that you also should do as I did to you."*

From today's scripture, how does **THE** Shepherd inspire **you** to shepherd **your** flock?

_____

_____

MINUTE OF MEDITATION
"Let everything that has breath praise the Lord. Praise the Lord"
(Psalm 150:6).

PRAYER
Adoration, **C**onfession, **T**hanksgiving, **S**upplication